Career Counseling

SKILLS AND TECHNIQUES
FOR PRACTITIONERS

Career Counseling

SKILLS AND TECHNIQUES
FOR PRACTITIONERS

Norman C. Gysbers
University of Missouri–Columbia

Earl J. Moore

PRENTICE-HALL, INC.
Englewood Cliffs, New Jersey 07632

Library of Congress Cataloging-in-Publication Data

Gysbers, Norman C.
  Career counseling.

  Bibliography: p.
  Includes index.
  1. Vocational guidance.   I. Moore, Earl J.
  II. Title.
  HF5381.C97   1987   331.7′02′07   86-16892
  ISBN 0-13-114562-2

Cover design: Wanda Lubelska
Manufacturing buyer: Barbara Kittle

Printed in the United States of America

10 9 8 7 6 5 4 3

ISBN   0-13-114562-2   01

Prentice-Hall International (UK) Limited, *London*
Prentice-Hall of Australia Pty. Limited, *Sydney*
Prentice-Hall of Canada Inc., *Toronto*
Prentice-Hall Hispanoamericana, S.A., *Mexico*
Prentice-Hall of India Private Limited, *New Delhi*
Prentice-Hall of Japan, Inc., *Tokyo*
Prentice-Hall of Southeast Asia Pte. Ltd., *Singapore*
Editora Prentice-Hall do Brasil, Ltda., *Rio de Janeiro*

In Memory of the Genius of

EARL J. MOORE

November 18, 1930–January 11, 1983

Contents

Preface

In your work in career counseling you may be searching for techniques to help you and your clients understand who they are and how they see themselves and their world. You may be looking for techniques to help you join with your clients to systematically gather, organize, and use such information in career planning and decision making. You may be seeking to enhance your skills to improve the career assessment, counseling, planning, and training and development activities that your school, agency, institution, or company provides.

The purpose of this book is to help you expand and extend the skills and techniques in your career counseling repertoire. Specifically, this book is designed to help you update and add to the skills and techniques that will help you to understand and interpret information gathered and behavior observed during career counseling. It is designed to help you understand and interpret information and behavior in terms of themes, or the ideas, beliefs, attitudes, and values clients hold about themselves, others, and the world in which they live. It will enable you to help clients to relate such information and behavior to career planning and decision making.

To help you gain these specific skills, this book brings together selected concepts and techniques from such diverse sources as marriage and family counseling, cognitive psychology, learning styles theory, and hemispheric functioning and applies them to the career counseling process. The techniques and the skills in using them are designed to complement and strengthen—not replace—your use of other career counseling techniques such as standardized tests and inventories and career and labor market information. In fact, skill in using the concepts and techniques described in this book can enhance your use of tests and information. This enhancement will result from the new insights both you and your clients can gain from these techniques about how to conceptualize and interpret test data and when and how to use career and labor market information.

The use of the selected concepts and techniques described in the book and the skills involved assumes that you have at least beginning knowledge of career development theories and practices, counseling theories and techniques, and tests and inventories in counseling. It is not a comprehensive overview of career counseling techniques. It is a book for individuals who already have a beginning theoretical and practice base in career counseling and want to update and expand their career counseling repertoires with concepts and techniques from the disciplines of marriage and family counseling and cognitive psychology. It is a book for individuals who want to update and expand their ability to gain insights into client behavior, to develop hypotheses about such behavior, and to apply this knowledge to the selection of career counseling techniques.

The Introduction provides a foundation on which rest the career counseling techniques that follow. We believe that techniques not related to and founded on an understanding of human growth and development are ineffective. Thus the Introduction provides you with a way of looking at human growth and development, called life career development, and offers a framework for the career counseling process.

To use the career counseling techniques that follow effectively and to relate them to other techniques that you may be using, you may need to learn or update a number of career counseling skills. These skills include ways to understand and interpret client information and client behavior and ways to analyze the life career themes clients use to organize and live their lives. Chapters 1 and 2 describe these skills in detail and provide you with examples so that you can see these skills in action.

Life career assessment (LCA) is presented in Chapter 3. It is a systematic way to collect meaningful client information in a reasonable amount of time. It is person-centered so that individuals also learn about themselves. The LCA helps you and your clients identify and understand the life career themes they use to live their lives. It also provides information that can serve as a springboard for additional career counseling or other career development activities.

Chapter 4, written especially for this book by Joseph T. Kunce and Corrine S. Cope, presents a technique called personal styles analysis. This technique integrates learning style information with personality characteristics. It will enable you to help your clients learn about a way to understand who they are, how their personality and learning styles relate, and, most important, how this knowledge may relate to education or occupational goals. It is useful for assessment center work and individual career planning and counseling activities in schools, agencies, and business and industry settings.

Chapter 5 introduces you to occupational card sorts in general and to the Missouri Occupational Preference Inventory in particular. You will learn about the usefulness of card sorts as a career counseling technique by learning how to use the Missouri Occupational Preference Inventory. The focus is on helping clients understand the life career themes they use to think about themselves and their present and future lives.

Chapter 6 enables you to help clients develop and use individual career plans. These plans are viewed as both instruments and processes that people can use by themselves or with others to create and manage their life careers. As instruments, career plans provide a place for people to record information about themselves: their aptitudes, interests, competencies, and achievements. They become organizers for personal and professional information that can be updated continually. As processes, plans become a pathway or guide through which individuals use past and present information to look to the future. Plans also can be used to aid in an individual's growth within an educational institution, agency, company, or organization through the more effective use of interests and abilities.

The last chapter, Chapter 7, presents an analysis and discussion of the career counseling process. The process is described in terms of two major phases: (1) client goal or problem identification, clarification, and specification and (2) client goal or problem resolution. Specific attention is given to how the skills and procedures presented in the previous chapters are integrated and used in the career counseling process.

Taken in total the seven chapters provide both a perspective for career counseling and a framework through which the specific career counseling skills and techniques presented in this book can be used to help you and your clients better understand themselves and their worlds.

Acknowledgments

Earl J. Moore, my friend, colleague, and co-author, died before the manuscript for this book was completed. At the time of his death Earl was an associate professor in the Department of Educational and Counseling Psychology at the University of Missouri–Columbia. We outlined the entire book together, and he conducted the research and provided the basic material for Chapters 1 and 2. Earl died on January 11, 1983.

I am indebted to the late Richard H. Johnson for his conceptualization of the basic structure of the life career assessment (LCA) presented in Chapter 3. Also, thanks to Robert L. Krick for his initial work on the LCA. In addition, I wish to thank Joseph T. Kunce and Corrine S. Cope for their excellent chapter on personal styles analysis (Chapter 4). This chapter was written especially for this book and presents for the first time Kunce's model of personal styles analysis and practical examples of its use in career counseling.

I also wish to thank James H. Straub for his permission to adapt material from the Missouri Occupational Preference Inventory Manual for use in Chapter 5 and Pamela M. Carlson for her contributions to the early development of the MOPI. Similarly, I wish to thank Randy McAlister for his permission to adapt and use material describing the career portfolio and the career passport in Chapter 6. In addition, thanks to Elsie Cafferty for her permission to use parts of her paper, "Learning Style as a Tool in Career Guidance," in Chapter 2. Finally, thanks to Mary J. Heppner for her insightful review and comments on the entire manuscript and to Marita S. Barkis for her comments on Chapter 7.

Introduction

CAREER COUNSELING: A PERSPECTIVE AND A FRAMEWORK

As we near the close of the twentieth century, the complexity of the world in which we live and work continues to increase. The technology explosion continues to have a substantial impact on the nature and structure of businesses, industries, and occupations. In turn, these changes affect who we are both as individuals and as members of society.

Vast and far-reaching changes are also occurring in the nature and structure of our social system. Our values and beliefs about ourselves and our society are changing, as are the ways we look at and understand our own development. People are looking for meaning in their lives, for a wholeness, particularly as they think about the work they do, their situation as a family member or as an individual, their involvement in their community, their role in continuing education, and their involvement in leisure activities.

Concurrently, and perhaps as a result of these changes, new and more holistic ways of looking at and understanding career behavior and development have emerged. The theory and research base of counseling psychology has expanded substantially during the past twenty years. Growth in the theory and research base of career psychology has been equally dramatic, resulting in the convergence of ideas from counseling

1

and career psychology concerning career behavior and development and the interventions to facilitate it.

The convergence of ideas has stimulated the development of a new array of career counseling techniques that are taking their place alongside traditional and time-honored career counseling techniques. These new techniques are emerging from this convergence through the application in career counseling of concepts from marriage and family counseling (Zingaro, 1983), cognitive behavioral psychology (Keller, Biggs, and Gysbers, 1982), personal styles theory (Pinkney, 1983), learning styles theory (Wolfe and Kolb, 1980), and theories based on hemispheric function.

This convergence of ideas has stimulated another look at the career counseling process itself and has alerted us to new ways to gather client information. Perhaps even more important, it has given us new ways to understand client information and behavior. It has also opened up new ways to apply these understandings through the interventions used to assist clients to understand their career behavior and to facilitate their career development.

To set the stage for the rest of the book, the first part of the Introduction presents a model that reflects the new and more holistic ways of looking at and understanding career behavior and development. In doing so, a perspective is provided that offers a philosophical foundation for the career counseling skills and techniques that follow. The second part of the Introduction outlines a framework for career counseling to help you relate and integrate the career counseling techniques presented in the subsequent chapters with your own career counseling style.

A PERSPECTIVE: THE CAREER-CONSCIOUS INDIVIDUAL

A model developed to reflect these new and more holistic ways of looking at and understanding human growth and development is the career-conscious individual model, which was conceptualized by Gysbers and Moore (1971, 1981). It is an outcome-oriented model designed to provide a comprehensive overview of the knowledge, skills, and attitudes (competencies) individuals need in order to facilitate their development. The concept of consciousness was taken from the work of Reich and his description of how consciousness functions in individuals.

> Included within the idea of consciousness is a person's background, education, politics, insight, values, emotions, and philosophy, but consciousness is more than these or even the sum of them. It is the whole man; his "head"; his way of life. It is that by which he creates his own life and thus creates the society in which he lives. (Reich, 1971, p. 15)

In helping individuals reach their potential we are stimulating career consciousness—the ability for individuals to visualize and plan their lives. The challenge for us is to create career consciousness in individuals: to help them project themselves into possible life roles, settings, and events; analyze these roles, settings, and events; and relate the findings to their present situations.

LIFE CAREER DEVELOPMENT

The career-conscious individual model is based on life career development concepts and principles. Life career development is defined as self-development over the life span through the integration of the roles, settings, and events in a person's life. The word *life* in the definition indicates that the focus of this conception of human growth and development is on the total person, the human career. The word *career* identifies and relates the many and often-varied roles in which individuals are involved (student, worker, consumer, citizen, parent); the settings in which individuals find themselves (home, school, work, community); and the events that occur over their lifetimes (entry job, marriage, divorce, retirement). The word *development* is used to indicate that individuals are always in process of becoming. When used in sequence, the words *life career development* bring these separate meanings together, but at the same time a greater meaning evolves. Life career development describes total, unique individuals, each with his or her own life-style (Gysbers and Moore, 1975).

In terms of life career development the word *career* has a substantially different meaning from some definitions. Here the focus is on *all* aspects of life as interrelated parts of the whole person.

During the 1970s substantial work was done in developing basic ideas and vocabulary to define career development in life terms. In the early 1970s Jones et al. (1972) defined career as encompassing a variety of possible patterns of personal choice related to an individual's total life-style, including occupation, education, personal and social behavior, learning how to learn, social responsibility (citizenship), and leisure activities. Super (1975, 1984) proposed a definition of career that involves the interaction of various life roles over the life span. He portrays these interactions in a concept called the life-career rainbow.

Wolfe and Kolb summed up the life view of career development:

Career development involves one's whole life, not just occupation. As such, it concerns the whole person, needs and wants, capacities and potentials, excitements and anxieties, insights and blindspots, warts and all. More than that, it concerns him/her in the ever-changing contexts of his/her life. The environmental pressures and constraints, the bonds that tie him/her to significant others, responsibilities to children and aging parents, the total structure of one's circumstances are also factors that must be understood and reckoned with. In these terms career development and personal development converge. Self and circumstance—evolving, changing, unfolding in mutual interaction—constitute the focus and the drama of career development. (Wolfe and Kolb, 1980, pp. 1–2)

It should be clear that the term *career*, when viewed from this broad perspective, is not a new word for *occupation*. People have careers; the work world or marketplace has occupations. Unfortunately, too many people use the word *career* when they should use the word *occupation*. The term *career* is not restricted to certain people. All people have a career; their life is their career. Finally, the words *life career development* do not delineate and describe only one part of human growth and development. Although it is useful to focus at times on different aspects of development—physical, emotional, and intellectual, for example—there is also a need to integrate these aspects. Life career development is advocated as an organizing and integrating concept for understanding and facilitating human growth and development (Gysbers and Moore, 1975, 1981).

IMPLICATIONS FOR CAREER COUNSELING

The broadened understanding of career development in life terms through such models as the career-conscious individual model makes it clear that we must respond to the developmental needs of people as well as to their crisis needs. Obviously, a crisis in a person's life must be dealt with, but crises are not the only emphasis in career counseling. Such thinking has many implications, as discussed below.

Prediction and Development

One implication revolves around the words *prediction* and *development*. Traditional practices emphasize the assessment of individuals' abilities and interests for the purpose of selecting an appropriate educational program or making an occupational choice. This emphasis, while important, is not sufficient. What is needed in addition is attention to life career development: providing through counseling the experiences to help the person explore and expand aptitudes and interests so that planning and decision making can be based on the broadest and most well-informed perspective possible. As Tennyson stated:

by concentrating upon assessment of abilities presumed to be related to choice outcomes, counselors have neglected to concern themselves with the development of abilities and aptitudes. While it is generally recognized that what a person is able to do depends to a considerable extent upon what he has learned or practiced, guidance personnel have been inclined to capitalize upon aptitudes already developed rather than cultivating new talents. (Tennyson, 1970, p. 262)

Treatment and Stimulus

Related to the prediction and development issue is the treatment and stimulus issue raised by Herr and Cramer (1979). They suggest that career counseling techniques can be used as a treatment response to problems already present. They also suggest that counseling practices can stimulate clients to acquire needed knowledge and skills to become more effective persons.

Deficits and Competencies

A major focus of career counseling is on helping people deal effectively with problems. Personal crises, a lack of information about training opportunities and the job market, and ineffective relationships with spouse, children, fellow employees, or supervisors are examples of problems to which counselors frequently are asked to respond. This focus must continue, and better ways of helping people with their problems must be found. In addition, a preventive focus is needed to help people develop and use their talents and competencies to create a better world for themselves and for society.

The preventive focus is not new. It has been a part of the counseling language and literature since the turn of the century. What is new is a sense of urgency about the importance of helping people develop and focus on their competencies rather than only on their deficits. Bolles (1981) developed an assessment technique to identify what he called functional/transferable skills. Although many people do not think of themselves as having any skills, everyone possesses a substantial number of skills, and their identification is an important part of positive growth and development.

Tyler suggests that our perceptions of people will change if they can develop as many competencies as possible.

> Competencies represent a completely different way of structuring our perceptions of others. The more competencies other people have the better for each of us, and it is essential for the functioning of a complex society that individuals develop different repertoires of competencies. The absolute limits of each person's living time make all-around competence for one individual impossible. We need one another. (Tyler, 1978, pp. 104–5)

A FRAMEWORK FOR CAREER COUNSELING

The purpose of the preceding discussion was not to establish dichotomies in career counseling practices among the various perspectives. The purpose was to point out the need to expand and extend our view of career counseling so that all of these perspectives can be included in our practices as we help people toward the goal of becoming competent, achieving individuals; as we help them become more active and involved in their own career planning and decision making.

What does the career counseling process look like that attempts to include and integrate all of these perspectives? A number of writers have described what is involved in the career counseling process beginning with Parsons (1909) and Williamson (1939, 1965) up to the present (Brooks, 1984; Crites, 1981; Kinnier and Krumboltz, 1984; Krumboltz, 1983; Reardon, 1984; Super, 1983, 1984). Of the contemporary writers, Crites, Kinnier and Krumboltz, and Super, in particular, have attempted to include and integrate perspectives such as these.

Crites (1981) describes the process of career counseling as involving diagnoses, problem clarification, problem specification, and problem resolution. He also suggests that making a career choice, the acquisition of decisional skills, and enhanced general adjustment are often seen as the goals of career counseling. Finally, he points out that to reach these goals, interview techniques, test interpretation, and occupational information are the methods generally used as the career counseling process unfolds.

Kinnier and Krumboltz (1984) focus on three basic phases in their model of career counseling: assessment, intervention, and evaluation. During the assessment phase the counselor and client work on relationship development, agreement about the structure of the counseling sessions, and agreement about the goals of counseling. Problem exploration and identification also are part of the assessment phase. Part of the counseling session involves identifying obstacles that clients need to overcome. The intervention phase consists of the activities that counselor and client think will help alleviate the client's concern or reach the client's goal. Finally, during the evaluation phase the client and counselor evaluate how well the interventions worked.

In an article published in 1983 Super makes the point that career assessment based on traditional methodology was useful but not sufficient to encourage, support, and help people become active career planners and decision makers. To counteract the insufficiencies found in traditional models, Super recommends that we consider a new model he calls the developmental assessment model. The model encompasses traditional methodology but also brings into focus work salience and career maturity. In addition, Super emphasizes the need to assist individuals in the assimulation of self- and environmental information. (An expanded version of Super's model was published in 1984.)

For purposes of this book, the career counseling process is envisioned as having two major phases and a number of subphases. In outline form it looks like this:

I. Client goal or problem identification, clarification, and specification
  A. Establishing a client-counselor relationship including client-counselor responsibilities
  B. Gathering client self- and environmental information to understand the client's goal or problem
     1. Who is the client?
        a. How does the client view himself or herself, others, and his or her world?
        b. What language does the client use to represent these views?
        c. What themes does the client use to organize and direct his or her behavior based on these views?
     2. What is the client's current status and environment like?
        a. Client's life roles, settings, and events
        b. Relationship to client's goal or problem
  C. Understanding client self- and environmental information by sorting, analyzing, and relating such information to client's goal or problem through the use of:
     1. Career development theories
     2. Counseling theories
     3. Classification systems
  D. Drawing conclusions; making diagnoses
II. Client goal or problem resolution
  A. Taking action; interventions selected based on diagnoses. Some examples of interventions include counseling techniques, testing, personal styles analyses, career and labor market information, individual career plans, occupational card sorts, and computerized information and decision systems.
  B. Evaluating the impact of the interventions used; did interventions resolve the client's goal or problem?
     1. If goal or problem was not resolved, recycle.
     2. If goal or problem was resolved, close counseling relationship.

Keep in mind that these phases may take place during one interview or may unfold over two or more interviews with clients. Also keep in mind that while these phases logically follow one another on paper, in actual practice they may not. There often is a back-and-forth flow to the process. Finally, not everyone who seeks help wants or needs to go through the full process of career counseling. Some may want only a little assistance, prefering instead to handle the remainder of the process alone.

The outline that has just been presented is designed to provide you with a framework to review and examine the selected career counseling skills and techniques presented in the chapters that follow for possible incorporation into your own career counseling style. The framework provides a context in which these career counseling skills and techniques can be examined and understood. In addition, the framework shows where these skills and techniques can fit into the career counseling process and can relate to your other skills and techniques. Finally, the framework helps show when and how these skills and techniques can be adapted or adopted for your use with clients.

8   *Introduction*

REFERENCES

BOLLES, R. N., *The Three Boxes of Life.* Berkeley, Calif.: Ten Speed Press, 1981.

BROOKS, L., "Career Counseling Methods and Practice," in *Career Choice and Development,* eds. D. Brown, L. Brooks, and Associates. San Francisco: Jossey-Bass, 1984.

CRITES, J. O., *Career Counseling: Models, Methods, and Materials.* New York: McGraw-Hill, 1981.

GYSBERS, N. C., and MOORE, E. J., "Career Development in the Schools," in *Contemporary Concepts in Vocational Education,* ed. G. F. Law. Washington, D.C.: American Vocational Association, 1971.

———, and ———, "Beyond Career Development—Life Career Development," *The Personnel and Guidance Journal,* 53 (1975), 647–52.

———, and ———, *Improving Guidance Programs.* Englewood Cliff, N.J.: Prentice-Hall, 1981.

HERR, E. L., and CRAMER, S. H. *Career Guidance Through the Life Span.* Boston: Little, Brown, 1979.

JONES, G. B., HAMILTON, J. A., GANSHOW, L. H., HELLIWELL, C. B., and WOLFF, J. M., *Planning, Developing, and Field Testing Career Guidance Programs: A Manual and Report.* Palo Alto, Calif.: American Institutes for Research, 1972.

KELLER, K. E., BIGGS, P. A., and GYSBERS, N. C. "Career Counseling from a Cognitive Perspective," *The Personnel and Guidance Journal,* 60 (1982), 376–71.

KINNIER, R. T., and KRUMBOLTZ, J. D., "Procedures for Successful Career Counseling," in *Designing Careers: Counseling to Enhance Education, Work, and Leisure,* eds. N. C. Gysbers and Associates. San Francisco: Jossey-Bass, 1984.

KRUMBOLTZ, J. D., *Private Rules in Career Decision Making.* Columbus, Ohio: National Center for Research in Vocational Education, 1983.

PARSONS, F., *Choosing a Vocation.* Boston: Houghton-Mifflin, 1909.

PINKNEY, J. W., "The Myers-Biggs Type Indicator as an Alternative in Career Counseling, *The Personnel and Guidance Journal,* 62 (1983), 173–77.

REARDON, R. C., "Use of Information in Career Counseling," in *Career Development Interventions.* eds. H. D. Burck and R. C. Reardon. Springfield, Ill.: Charles C Thomas, 1984.

REICH, C. A., *The Greening of America.* New York: Bantam Books, 1971.

SUPER, D. E., "Emergent Decision Making in a Changing Society," in *Proceedings of the International Seminar on Educational and Vocational Guidance.* Lisbon: Portuguese Psychological Society, 1975.

———, "Assessment in Career Guidance: Towards Truly Developmental Counseling," *The Personnel and Guidance Journal,* 61 (1983), 555–62.

TENNYSON, W., "Comment," *The Vocational Guidance Quarterly,* 18 (1970), 261–63.

TYLER, L., *Individuality, Human Possibilities and Personal Choice in the Psychological Development of Men and Women.* San Francisco, Calif.: Jossey-Bass, 1978.

WILLIAMSON, E. G., *Vocational Counseling.* New York: McGraw-Hill, 1965.

———, *How to Counsel Students.* New York: McGraw-Hill, 1939.

WOLFE, D. M., and KOLB, D. A., "Career Development, Personal Growth, and Experimental Learning," in *Issues in Career and Human Resource Development,* ed. J. W. Springer. Madison, Wis.: American Society for Training and Development, 1980.

ZINGARO, J. C., "A Family Systems Approach for the Career Counselor," *The Personnel and Guidance Journal,* 62 (1983), 24–27.

CHAPTER 1

Understanding
and Interpreting
Client Information
and Behavior

As evidence mounts regarding the interrelationship between human cognitions and emotional arousal, counselors must be concerned with how clients think about themselves and the crucial events in their lives. Literally, what clients say to themselves may be the crucial mediating processes in their lives. (Blocher, 1980, p. 335)

As suggested in the framework for career counseling described in the Introduction, a major task in career counseling, once you have begun to establish the client-counselor relationship and responsibilities, is to gather client self- and environmental information to help identify, clarify, and specify the client's goal or problem. What is the client's goal or problem? Who is the client? How does the client view himself or herself? What language does the client use to represent these views? What are the client's current status and environment like? As answers to these and similar questions are forthcoming, the following questions arise. What does this information mean? How do you interpret it? And, finally, how do you use your interpretations (diagnoses) with clients to help them take action to respond to their goals or problems?

With some clients the process of gathering, understanding, and using such information and behavior in career counseling is straightforward. No defensiveness or evasiveness is present. However, for other clients, whether by conscious choice or unconscious action, defensiveness and evasiveness become part of the career counseling process and must be addressed. For still other clients, irrational beliefs and distorted thinking permeate their views of self and the career planning and decision-making process. Personality dynamics, irrational beliefs, motivational issues, and distorted thinking can often short-circuit the best use of tools and techniques in career counseling. To be effective you will need to learn how to address these issues before much progress can be made with such clients.

How are defensiveness and evasiveness in clients to be understood? What is the impact of irrational beliefs and distorted thinking? What skills are needed to respond to such information and behavior? For purposes of this book we will focus on nine skills that will help you understand and work with clients who exhibit these and similar behaviors in career counseling.

These skills are as follows:

1. Using presuppositions
2. Using embedded questions and directives
3. Correcting transformational errors
4. Labeling and reframing
5. Recognizing and dealing with resistance
6. Identifying irrational beliefs
7. Identifying distorted thinking
8. Using reflective judgment stages
9. Focusing on excuses

USING PRESUPPOSITIONS

Presupposition usage is defined as the use of assumptions (Bandler, Grinder, and Satir, 1976). You assume or presuppose a client's behavior. You do *not* ask if the behavior exists; it is presupposed that the client already exhibits the behavior. Since the behavior is already approved, specifics and feelings can be related without a yes-no value judgment. Here are some examples:

NO ASSUMPTIONS	PRESUPPOSITIONS
Do you like your work?	What are some things you like about your work?
	What do you dislike about your work?
How do you get along with your supervisor?	What kind of supervisors are best for you?
	What do supervisors do that you dislike?

In the above examples the following assumptions were made in the presupposition statements:

· All people like something about their work.
· All people dislike something about their work.
· There are supervisor characteristics that facilitate job satisfaction.
· There are supervisor characteristics that do not facilitate job satisfaction.

The structuring of presuppositions may take many forms. In the above examples a presupposition regarding the polarity of feelings toward objects is established—all people have *likes* and *dislikes* about objects. The like-dislike approach suggests fairness and equality.

In other instances simple directives are appropriate: "What are your plans?" not, "Do you have plans?" A focus on a *process* may be called for: "Please describe your process of deciding to seek career counseling," not, "Did you go through a process of deciding to come here?" The next skill discussed, that of asking embedded questions and giving directives, supports presupposition usage.

USING EMBEDDED QUESTIONS AND DIRECTIVES

Embedded questions and directives are used in everyday relationships. For example, the phone rings while you are in your friend's home and your friend glances at you and says, "Can you answer the phone?" This statement is a simple question that requires only a "yes" or "no" answer, yet the typical response to it is to answer the phone. The request has the force of a command. In other words, you respond to this question as though your friend had made a direct request of you to answer the phone. The use of the yes/no form of a question in cases such as this is the polite way of making a direct request (Bandler, Grinder, and Satir, 1976).

The interview skill is to use questions that are not really questions in the usual sense; they are really polite commands. Note the following questions/commands: "Can you tell me specifically what you . . . ?" "I'm curious whether you can . . . ?" Conversely, we can embed questions in a language form that does not demand an answer, yet begins the process of bringing certain issues to the attention of the person listening. Notice these examples: "I'm wondering what it is that you . . . ?" "I don't know whether the job . . . was easy or difficult . . . ?" "I'm curious whether you can shed some light . . . ?" This form of questioning opens up the maximum number of choices about how and when to respond. Clients feel free to respond rather than being forced or commanded, since they are providing assistance rather than answers. This is best illustrated by the counselor who uses such statements as, "I am having trouble understanding how it happened. I am mixed up. Maybe you can help me by. . . ." Most counselors have learned to use such statements accompanied by nonverbal gestures that support wondering and struggling such as frowns and deep breaths.

CORRECTING TRANSFORMATIONAL ERRORS*

Three types of transformational errors often occur in career counseling: information errors, limitation errors, and logic errors. Information errors can occur because language, at best, provides only an approximate description of actual feelings and experiences of clients. Limitation errors can occur because clients often focus attention on only one aspect of an experience or feeling. Logic errors can occur because client thinking processes may be distorted.

Information Errors

Career counseling clients sometimes make errors as they relate relevant information about themselves and their world. These errors are deletion, references to unspecified persons, use of unspecified verbs, referential indexing, and modal operators. It is important for you to recognize these errors so that you can respond accordingly.

Deletion.   Deletion takes place when an important aspect of an experience is omitted. For example, during a counseling session a client might say, "I'm inadequate." An appropriate question to ask is, "To do what?" Such a question will help focus on what the client has omitted. Here are several other examples:

CLIENT STATEMENTS	COUNSELOR QUESTIONS
"My thinking is better."	"About what?" "Better than what?"
"My supervisor says I'm not responsible."	"Responsible about what?"

References to Unspecified Persons.   This error is the result of the vague use of general nouns or pronouns. In a counseling session a client might say, "They don't understand me." Here you might respond, "Who doesn't understand you?" The focus is on trying to determine to whom the word *they* refers. Here are some additional examples:

CLIENT STATEMENTS	COUNSELOR QUESTIONS
"People get me down."	"Who specifically?"
"I'm not able to cope."	"With what?" "With whom?"

---

* Some of the material on information errors, limitation errors, and logic errors is adapted from G. J. Rath and K. S. Stoyanoff, "Understanding and Improving Communication Effectiveness," in *The 1982 Annual for Facilitators, Trainers, and Consultants,* eds. J. William Pfeiffer and Leonard D. Goodstein (San Diego, Calif.: University Associates, Inc., 1982), pp. 166–73. Used with permission.

Use of Unspecified Verbs.   A client using unspecified verbs might say, "My supervisor ignores me." You might ask for clarification by saying, "Specifically what does your supervisor do that makes you feel ignored?"

CLIENT STATEMENTS	COUNSELOR QUESTIONS
"It goes against what I believe."	"Explain how this happens."
"I'm blocked in making a decision about moving."	"How are you blocked?"

Referential Indexing.   The fourth type of information error, referential indexing, occurs when a client introduces a person, place, or thing into a sentence but is not specific. For example, your client says, "I'm just not sure." A temptation for you at this point may be to fill in your own understanding of what your client may not be sure about, thereby losing the opportunity to learn what your client thinks. Overcome this temptation and ask, "What specifically are you not sure about?" Responses that are effective for ascertaining the referential index include such statements as, "Can you be more specific?" "Can you give me some examples?" "For instance?" "Such as?" The following are some examples of referential indexing:

CLIENT	MISSING PIECE	COUNSELOR
"The work was boring."	What's boring	"What made the work boring?"
"I don't know."	Know what	"What don't you know?"
"I am confused."	Confused about what	"You are confused about what?"
"Things get me down."	What things	"Describe the things."

Modal Operators.   Some clients' model of the world is limited by modal operators such as, "But I just can't" or "I'm being forced to . . ." (Bandler, Grinder, and Satir, 1976). These words express limits. To free clients from these modal operators that limit choice, mild confrontation is directed toward identifying the specific limiting factors. Modal operators usually consist of two types: possibility and necessity.

POSSIBILITY	COUNSELOR CONFRONTATION
"Unable to, can't."	"What stops you?"
"Impossible, must not."	"What would happen if . . . ?"

NECESSITY	COUNSELOR CONFRONTATION
"Have to, necessary."	"What would happen if . . . ?"
"Must, no choice."	"You did?" or "If you don't."

We recommend that you challenge these client cue words and phrases. When you do, the client may have difficulty accepting responsibility for encountering his or her problems. Therefore, some resistance can be expected. A client may respond to "What stops you?" with "I really don't know." You can then ask the client to guess. Asking people to guess relieves them of the pressure to know accurately, and therefore they often come up with relevant material. A request to guess when clients claim not to know invariably produces answers. The answers tell us a great deal about how clients organize their experiences, what resources they may have available, and what limits they accept.

In summary, information error correction is the process of assisting clients to be specific. When you hear something that you are unable to connect to your own experience, rather than letting unsuccessful communication slide by or pretending that you understand or that you can read your client's mind, simply identify the portion of the statement that you do not understand and ask about it. Any assumptions you may have need to be checked out. By requesting clear communication, you give clients the message that they need to take seriously both their ability to understand and their ability to communicate and that you are interested in *really* understanding what they may want.

Limitation Errors

Some clients with whom you work have a limited view of the opportunities and choices available to them because they focus on only one aspect of an experience. They can limit their view in three ways: by using universal qualifiers, by assuming certain situations are impossible, and by assuming that things are inevitable.

Universal Qualifiers. In career counseling you may find that some clients use words such as *always, never, all, every,* and *nobody.* Such statements imply that things are true without exception. It is unlikely, however, that things are without exception. Thus when a client says, "I always do that," you may question, "Do you do that in every single case?" This may help your client see the fallacy in such statements.

Assuming Impossibility. When clients use such words as *can't, impossible, must not,* and *unable to,* they are placing limits on their own ability to bring about change. For example, your client may say, "I can't talk with my boss." Your response might be, "You haven't found a way yet to talk to your boss." Or, more directly, you may say, "You may not want to talk to your boss."

Presuming Inevitability.   This error is exactly the opposite of the previous error. Here your clients may use such words as *have to, necessary, must, no choice,* and *forced to.* Suppose a client said, "I disagreed with my boss so much that I had no choice but to resign." You could respond by saying, "You chose not to have any choices. You could have worked with your boss to resolve the situation or you could have just accepted the disagreement as normal. Actually, you had a lot of choices that you chose not to consider."

Logic Errors

Logic errors are those in which clients make statements that establish illogical relationships, which in turn lead to ineffective communication. There are three logic error types that you may find your clients using in career counseling. They are faulty cause-and-effect statements, mind reading, and unlimited generalization.

Faulty Cause-and-Effect Statements.   Faulty cause-and-effect statements are made by clients who believe that one person's behavior can be the direct physical cause of another person's change. They may claim that they have no control over an experience, which then literally makes them have the experience. The cause-and-effect pattern goes something like this: "This caused that, thus, I am helpless. It is final." This type of thinking is evident in the statement: "The boss really makes me upset." Typically, clients who make such statements do not feel that they have choices or control and, hence, responsibility over their own lives. You may need to assist your clients to recognize choices by asking them to describe in detail the process by which someone *causes* them to feel or sense what they are experiencing. You could begin by asking, "What specifically does your boss do that upsets you? Can you give me some examples?"

Mind Reading.   A client may draw conclusions about someone else's thoughts or feelings without directly talking with that person. Mind reading occurs in any situation in which one person claims to know the inner experience of another without receiving a direct communication of the second person's experience. For example, a client may state, "I know that my supervisor is unhappy with me." By replying, "How do you know, specifically, that your supervisor is unhappy with you?" the focus will be on specific behavioral cues that your client is using, sometimes wrongly, to come to a conclusion.

Unlimited Generalization.   Unlimited generalizations are personal opinions that are stated as if they pertain to everyone. "It's a good idea to talk about your feelings" is an example of such a statement. You could respond with, "For whom is it a good idea to talk about feelings?"

LABELING AND REFRAMING

Labeling and reframing (Bandler and Grinder, 1979; Harman and O'Neill, 1981) clients' expressions provide a way to help them see themselves and their world differently. By providing new words and ways of organizing those words, you can help your clients with new patterns for organizing and viewing their world. Motivation and attitudinal changes often are associated with the labeling and reframing processes.

A change of frame is a primary event. A change of label is a secondary consequence. Reframing is a change in the frame of reference we use to look at some particular behavior, such as a moral perspective versus a medical perspective or an individual-personal view versus a family systems view. Relabeling should be reserved for those instances in which there is a change in label with no change in frame of reference, for example, neurotic versus psychotic. Both labels remain in the medical framework.

An excellent example of reframing occurred in Mark Twain's *Tom Sawyer*. Tom was able to reframe the painting of a white fence from something that was work and undesirable to something that was fun and desirable. His friends accepted his reframing of the task and proceeded to join in painting the fence enthusiastically. This does not mean that all reframing is controlling, but it does provide a different perception that suggests new behavioral responses to an old stimulus.

Labeling and relabeling skills are aimed at extracting your clients' experiences and bringing them to their attention with new verbal descriptions that punctuate their importance. Bolles (1985) does this when he helps people identify their functional job skills. He asks individuals to describe something that they do well. He then relabels these descriptions as functional job skills. For example, being a good mother and taking care of children is labeled as the functional skill of caring for people and helping others. The homemaker role is divided into various functional skills that can be relabeled as functional skills transferable to other jobs or roles. Labels provide a focus. When clients are considering career decisions, their experiences may need to be relabeled in terms of functional job skills. Academic skills often are relabeled but social skills, leisure skills, and survival skills are sometimes overlooked.

Relabeling and reframing focus on the positive aspects of the individual. The emphasis is on what persons can do and the competencies they possess. For individuals who typically are described as having a low self-concept, relabeling and reframing techniques can be crucial and may need to be accented continually.

Reframing consists of a change of perception that implies a behavioral response that will be different or accented. This also may involve a change of values. A con artist and a salesperson have many of the same skills. Negatively described behavior often contains skills needed for survival. For example, reframing the ability to read nonverbal cues may allow the con artist to be successful. These skills also are valuable for a salesperson. Negatives can sometimes be reframed as positives.

Reframing also can be used to confront clients. A paradoxical situation can be created with resistant and unmotivated clients. Inappropriate classroom behavior may be reframed as a means of getting revenge and showing one's power so that the person will feel worthwhile. It is advantageous to reframe descriptions that are not behavioral into behavioral statements. This allows for specifying and interpretation.

An effective technique using labeling and reframing ideas is *paradoxical intention*. It is especially helpful with clients who exhibit behavior that involves considerable anticipatory anxiety as in the case with speech or performance anxiety (for example, job interview anxiety). In many instances clients feel that they have no control, and they resist taking responsibility for their actions. This technique can be used to break up destructive behavior patterns so that they can be replaced with behavior that is similar in pattern but positive in results.

In the accompanying chart twelve principles of paradoxical intention (McKay, Davis, and Fanning, 1981) are presented as a guide. You may not use all of them with every client or use them in the order presented; several steps may be going on concurrently in the career counseling process.

GUIDELINES FOR PARADOXICAL INTENTION*

PRINCIPLE	EXPLANATION
1. Forget understanding.	Understanding and insight often serve as a means of avoiding change.
2. Determine the symptom-solution cycle.	Ask the client the following: · What are you afraid of experiencing? Write it down using one word. · When does this behavior occur? · Where does this behavior occur? · How long does it last? · Who is around when it occurs? · What exactly do you do? · What exactly do you say to yourself?

* Adapted from M. McKay, M. Davis, and P. Fanning, *Thoughts and Feelings: The Art of Cognitive Stress Intervention* (Richmond, Calif.: New Harbinger Publications, 1981), pp. 180–88. Used with permission.

	• What reasons do you give for this behavior? • How do you feel when you do this behavior?
3. Encourage resistance.	Tell client to hold back disclosure of information. Tell client to go slow.
4. Define goal behavior.	List five ways in which you would be willing to have your problem behavior change. A checklist might be used to stimulate alternatives. Write down a statement describing your desired positive behavior.
5. Secure a commitment to change.	Create a "devil's pact": • Tell client you have a plan to solve the problem. • You agree to tell plan *only* if client agrees to follow plan regardless of its demands. • Tell client the plan will not be harmful. • Ask for an immediate decision (give client a few days at most). Imply no help without commitment. • Write a contract.
6. Set a time limit.	Ask client to set own deadline or time period for change. Give choice between a fast or slow method.
7. Describe the symptom.	Refer to symptom cycle in item 2. Make out a paradoxical prescription. • I will (describe behavior). • Add where, when, how long, with whom, and the usual sequence.
8. Include a variation.	Go back and change at least one, but no more than two, elements in the paradoxical prescription. Add something, take away something, or vary something.
9. Reframe in the client's language.	Use the client's "metaphor" to describe the paradoxical procedure. Because the paradox allows clients to do what they were trying not to do, they may find the directives humorous.
10. Secure agreement to follow instructions.	Make sure the client understands your instructions and agrees to follow them. Have client record results.

11. Predict a relapse.	Have the client relapse into the old pattern of behavior at least once. He or she can compare feelings of the "old" and "new" behavior. Predict a relapse. "Don't be surprised if your problem crops up again next week or in a month."
12. Demystify or disengage.	If the problem behavior is eliminated, explain what you did. However, it may be a waste of time to explain it to some clients—let the process remain mysterious.

RECOGNIZING AND DEALING WITH RESISTANCE

In your career counseling you have worked with or will work with resistant or unmotivated clients. To work with such clients you need to recognize and understand the purpose of resistance and have some techniques ready to respond to it and deal with it. What follows is a description of what may be behind a client's resistance. In addition, you will find some suggested techniques to use to deal with resistance or the lack of motivation.

Recognizing Resistance: Fear of Taking Responsibility

The fear of taking responsibility may be behind client resistance. Acceptance of responsibility for decisions is one of the most difficult things we face in our lives. The counselor's awareness and appreciation of the potential burden and threat that taking responsibility represents to the client are prerequisite to dealing with resistance in a positive manner. In his treatment of clients Low discovered that anything sounds more hopeful and more comforting than the bleak prospect of having to undergo training in self-discipline. "Even brain tumors, mental ailments and hereditary 'taints' are preferable to that dreadful indictment as being a weak character and needing training in self-control" (Low, 1966, p. 279). Some pain is only temporary; however, the fear of being unable to perform hits directly at a client's self-worth and the inability to adequately determine one's existence. This presents the ominous prospect of continual, everlasting pain. Insulation and manipulation become necessary for survival.

Defense mechanisms and sabotaged communication serve as safeguards of self-esteem. This allows for an evasion of life tasks. It is always possible to collect more or less plausible reasons to justify escape from facing the challenges of life. We often do not realize what we are doing. Some strategies are intended to ensure against failure, exposure, or other catastrophes. The strategy used may have the effect of making it impossible for a client to meet an onerous responsibility—or at least it may delay the "moment of truth." Clients may try to disqualify themselves from a race they do not wish to run. If the race must be run, can failure be justified?

Defense Mechanisms.   Basic defense mechanisms are familiar. However, we are just beginning to appreciate the subtle and complex ways people use various strategies in adjusting to threatening conditions. For example, a subtle strategy we all use is called buying double insurance. No matter what the outcome, one can afford to take a partial chance because the safety of the individual is secured. Perhaps you can remember a report that you kept putting off and then just before the deadline, you worked feverishly, completed it, and turned it in at the last minute. By doing so you ensured your self-worth: If your supervisor did not like the report, it was because you did not have enough time to do an adequate job. If your supervisor did like it, you proved your unusual superiority.

This strategy is even more complex in an academic environment that places value on superior performance. The problem presented is described often as an inability to concentrate on school studies. The real problem occurs with some students who may not dare to attempt a true test of their intellectual capacity. The strategy used is buying insurance against the failure of being of ordinary intellect. According to Shulman and Mosak*:

> Such students are overly ambitious and demand that they be on top. They cannot afford to take the chance that their best efforts may leave them in the average range of their class. At first they make resolutions to study and indeed fantasize that they will study exceedingly well and do much outside reading on the subject. But they rarely do the necessary work. In a few weeks they are behind, and the chances for doing well are diminishing. Now they feel disappointed in themselves and even less inclined to study. People who want to be on top have no interest in studying hard to achieve only an average passing grade. This is shown in their procrastination, inability to concentrate, and restlessness when they begin to study. Throughout this unproductive activity they maintain a feeling of intellectual superiority. Trouble with studying and poor grades are blamed on bad habits, nervousness, lack of discipline, dull teachers, or uninteresting courses. Such students console themselves with the thought that they are really bright but are just unproductive for the moment. If only they were able to study properly, they would be at the top of the class. If they should happen to get high grades in spite of not studying, that is all to the good. They may even boast, "I never opened a book." If a poor grade is received, it is not because they are stupid, but because they are lazy. In our society most people would prefer to be regarded as lazy rather than stupid.

As a last resort such students may recall their earlier IQ scores and tell themselves that they are bright and could make good grades if they really

* Adapted from B. H. Shulman and H. H. Mosak, "Various Purposes of Symptoms, *Journal of Individual Psychology,* 23, no. 1 (1967), 82. Used with permission of the University of Texas Press.

wanted to. A high IQ score allows them to maintain their superiority without having to take academic risks.

Sabotaged Communication. We are educated at an early age not to venture or risk statements that might eventually be proved wrong or described as foolish. We learn how to avoid "owning" statements. Very often during a discussion statements of obvious belief are prefaced by, "Don't you think . . . ?" We frequently use the words *you* and *it* to direct ownership away from ourselves in conversations. Owning is threatening.

There is an advantage to mystifying situations so that there is always room for doubt and, therefore, justified inactivity. If the situation gets too threatening, one can always justify gracious withdrawal. Keeping communication incomplete allows for the freedom to do what one pleases.

Some communication tactics that allow the individual to maintain freedom from commitment and responsibility follow (Low, 1966).

Literalness. Rejecting of a statement made by another without opposing it openly is a device that can be used to block efforts, combat views, or reject suggestions by means of misinterpretation of the words the other person uses. The following is a situation that represents this sabotage approach:

CLIENT: I have been working on the behavior contract for several weeks and I don't see any results.
COUNSELOR: You must not be discouraged.
CLIENT: I am not discouraged. But of course if no one sees progress. . . .

Discrediting. Acceptance of the validity of another person's statement may imply one's own intellectual and moral inadequacy. Should the counselor's statement be fully accepted, the client's simplicity or stupidity is thereby implied. The tactic of discrediting ensures that the process of change does not proceed too fast or too far. A position of no obligation is maintained by using a verbal pattern of "but-knocking." But-knockers acknowledge the premise and then proceed to attack or deny its applicability to their situation.

COUNSELOR: Here is an outline of a conflict resolution procedure that has been used successfully in a number of companies.
CLIENT: Very interesting. I can see how it would work with those large West Coast companies, but our company is quite different.

Disparaging the Competence or Method. The client must prove that the counselor is qualified and unqualified, expert and inept, proficient and unskilled, all at the same time. The dilemma is solved by a simple trick: the counselor's competence is asserted explicitly but solidly denied by implication. The client's conscience is saved. For example, a client who consults a counselor on improving his ability to handle stress may demonstrate trust by continuing visits but uses phrases with disparaging implications, thus denying his ability to be helped.

CLIENT: My uncle was telling me about a new stress reduction technique . . . it seems to work for him . . . there must be something. . . .

Tactics of this kind permit the client to maintain the illusion of cooperation while at the same time disrupting or opposing the process. If the counseling process does not work, the method used or the counselor's incompetence was at fault, neither of which was the client's responsibility.

Challenging the Implication.   The implication of the interpretative statement may suggest a goal that could be perceived by the client as unrealistic or impossible to achieve. The reaction indicates skepticism and not full acceptance of a goal. Even though one accepts the basic sense of the statement, the pledge is given with reservations, which are evident in expressions such as, "I'll try my best." The client's "best" in such a case is nothing but a weak half effort, lukewarm cooperation, and the intent to give up should the first trial prove unsuccessful. To "try" means not to perform wholeheartedly. Without full acceptance of the goal, there is no all-out effort or risk.

Challenging Accountability.   A common rejection of pursuing further exploration is the recourse to heredity. No one on any account can be held responsible for a difficulty inherited from one's ancestors ("No one in our family does well in math."). Accountability also can be directed toward other sources such as unique temperaments and moods, past traumatic experiences, and metaphysical or religious experiences. By presenting a "hopeless" situation, the client takes no responsibility. Labeling is one way to support this type of thinking. After all, what can be expected from a "dyslexic" child or a "mental patient"?

Helplessness Is Not Hopelessness

Clients who feel helpless often will generate emotions of frustration: fear, anger, despair, envy, indignation, and disgust (Low, 1966). The result will be hopelessness unless responsibilities are shared.

1. Feelings of helplessness can be understood and used as a basis for action.
2. Expressions of hopelessness must be redirected toward a willingness to participate.
3. The way that responsibility will be shared must be described.
4. Evidence of commitment of time and effort must be provided.

5. The intervention/facilitation program must be broken down into small steps in a manner to assure motivation and perseverance.

Dealing with Resistance

Resistive or unmotivated clients have their own unique, idiosyncratic patterns for survival. Learning how to recognize these patterns is an important but often neglected part of career counseling. It is important because understanding these patterns will aid you in determining the next step you may take to assist your clients. Although there are no strategies that are guaranteed to clear away resistance or to motivate, there are a number of strategies that may be helpful. We suggest that you consider the following four approaches to deal with resistance:

1. Going back to the basics of correcting for *transformational errors*
2. *Joining* the client to enhance the counseling relationship
3. Using *metaphors* to minimize the threat and suggest alternatives
4. Applying *confrontation* in a purposeful manner

Transformational Errors. Focusing on transformational errors of clients may help negate negative self-talk and the avoidance patterns in which clients are sometimes involved. Remember that the problem of assuming responsibility is the underlying threat. As you identify the specifics of the threat, a concrete plan of action can be developed. After a plan has been developed, use the structure of the plan as an intervenor to your client's resistance pattern.

Joining. Joining is more than empathy, the reflection of feeling, or other relationship concepts associated with client-centered counseling. To join with individuals you must be able to appreciate their life struggles, not just the feelings of the moment. The feelings in the immediate setting may or may not be part of the joining process. When you join with clients, you let them know that you are aware of their total life struggles. To do this you can draw on your own experiences and wisdom that relate to roles, stages, and events that structure the tasks of life. Each individual is faced with different responsibilities as he or she moves through life. Each brings a unique response to common life-role and task responsibilities. You may need to relate a client's career change dilemmas to other aspects of his or her life, such as parenting an adolescent, an unexpected illness, or a financial crisis. What is it like to be eight years old, twenty-six years old, forty-five years old? Can you respect the power of such responses as depression, alcoholism, and delusions? This must be done in the context of daily living problems and career decision making. Ultimately, you will need to identify the client's areas of pain, difficulty, or stress and acknowledge that, although they cannot be avoided, you will respond to them sensitively.

Joining is letting your clients know that you understand them. It is letting them know that you are working with and for them. Only under this protection can clients have the security to explore alternatives, try the unusual, and change. You need to cross over the line to join with your clients to help them accept the responsibilities of their daily struggles. Your position is that of an active but neutral listener. You help your clients tell their story.

As soon as possible you should start working with your client's strengths. Focusing on weaknesses and negative barriers is not very fruitful. By confirming what is positive about your client, you become a source of self-esteem. Look for and emphasize positive functioning while pursuing goals of change. It is important that you be nonjudgmental about previous attempts to cope. Even when an obviously negative situation is discussed, your clients should not feel that they are being criticized or being made to feel guilty. Acknowledge that you have received the message: "You seem to be engaged in a continuous struggle. . . ." Stress that you are willing to work with them on the problem. When there is a feeling of partnership, joining has been accomplished.

Metaphors. The use of metaphor techniques in career counseling has become very involved in some circles, almost requiring the user to be a combination poet, linguist, choreographer, and biofeedback specialist. Our intent, however, is to accent the simple and straightforward aspects of the use of metaphors. In doing so we will focus on storytelling and retorts that stimulate reframing. We want to bring attention to stories, anecdotes, and idioms as communication devices to use with reluctant, resistive, and naive clients. Fundamentally, through metaphoric techniques we can confront someone with a problem that can be solved in some way. The solution arrived at may not be the only solution, but it can be one possible solution. The way the problem is solved can provide a solution for others in a similar circumstance. The characters and the story experience must be directly related to the client's problem. Examples of the sources of such stories include poems, novels, poetry, fairy tales, fables, parables, songs, movies, jokes, TV commercials, and gossip.

Gordon (1978) states that metaphors are a way of talking about experience. Listeners will take what is heard and relate it in terms of their own experience. As this is occurring, they may gain insight into their concerns. Experiences of the past become infused with the person's present model of the world. In addition, this new representation provides the counselor and client with a mutually understandable way of discussing present problems. The purpose underlying storytelling is that another person's experiences in overcoming a similar problem will suggest to the client either directly or indirectly ways to deal with his or her own situation. A counselor can present a story about a previous client who had a similar problem. The other client's problem should have a resolution similar to the kind that is needed with the present client. Even if the resolution does not quite fit, the client will see that a resolution may be possible and perhaps may begin searching for one. As long as the metaphor and problem are structurally similar, the client will consciously or unconsciously relate to them. Once the client's problem is identified with the story line, the client is free to incorporate, use, or reject the resolution offered.

It may seem paradoxical but the most effective use of metaphors results from a combination of spontaneity and planfulness. Spontaneity allows for a natural integration of material. The quality of presentation usually is better because the flow is less inhibited. However, the content of a metaphor must be short and to the point, and this requires a degree of planfulness that provides structure and a degree of simplicity that helps avoid doubt and confusion.

The more formal sources already have a built-in structure. In many cases it becomes a matter of casting the characters and then punctuating the storyline for effect. The less formal material is often derived from personal sources. It is not unusual to refer to one's own experiences. Reference to successful methods used by other clients also works. Personalizing material often is a great motivator.

Another major source for metaphor material is the universal experiences that are common to almost all people. For example, a child's struggle and ultimate success in learning to tie his shoestrings are parts of a universal challenge-success experience. The first day of school, the first date, and other common first-time experiences can provide both structure and personalization. You may wish to have a set of "universals" that you can use with common problems.

What follows are some sample metaphors. The first metaphor was used with a client who was afraid to leave home for a job offer in another community. The second metaphor was used with a client who was always excusing himself from taking responsibility because of a previous illness. The third metaphor was used with a client who often let play interfere with work.

METAPHOR 1

Because you grow plants in your house, you will understand my concern. I had this cluster of plants in a large pot. They seemed to be getting along all right. I watered them and took care of them, but they didn't seem to have a healthy look. They were crowded together. So in spite of their apparent satisfactory survival, they didn't seem to be able to grow. I decided to separate them into several pots. I repotted them. At first they looked kind of lonely and puny. But after proper care, they began to grow. They did not have to share the water and nutrients in the common pot. Now they had their own pots. Even the plant I left in the original pot prospered. Everything grew better. Eventually, they were all equally strong and prospering. It may be difficult to imagine how a cluster of plants can be divided and then each one become a strong separate potting. But it happened to me.

METAPHOR 2

There was this excellent baseball player. He was an outfielder and his specialty was hitting and stealing bases. One day an unfortunate accident occurred. He was running from first base to third base and had to slide into third base. His cleats caught on the turf and he broke his leg. He went through a long rehabilitation process. During part of the process, he developed a limp, but gradually all traces of the broken leg disappeared. He seemed to be able to run almost as fast, but in the back of his head he wondered if he had lost speed. He went back to playing baseball. There were no apparent signs of the injury—except on those occasions when he would ground the ball to the infield and be thrown out at first base. He would limp after he crossed first base and returned to the dugout. Ironically, he did not limp when he got a hit and roared into second base with a double.

METAPHOR 3

Life is a business. Granted there ought to be time in everybody's routine to play, to amuse oneself with games, and to divert attention from the serious aspects of the business of living. Nevertheless, life is not a game; it is a business that must be toiled at and attended to. Its business is to create and maintain values (family, community, education, religion, sociability). To play with the business of life means to gamble.

If you start a game, you are not obligated to continue it. You may drop it because you don't like it or because it bores you or because luck is against you or because you have a headache. Conversely, if you engage in business (job, marriage, the rearing of children, helping a friend, civic activities) you are under obligations to continue it, to see it through, to finish what you have started. Headaches, boredom, dislike, and strain are no justification for shirking the duty you have assumed or the commission you have accepted. Games are personal inclinations; business is group obligation. Games are pleasures, business is a task. A task may be pleasing, which means that pleasure and task can be combined. But if a game, no matter how pleasurable it is, interferes with the serious task of business, the thing to do is to stop the game and to continue the business. Tasks must have unquestioned priority over games. In life, even a plain conversation with a neighbor acquires the character of a task. It imposes the obligation to be courteous, to be friendly, to show humility, to create good will, and to avoid criticism and intellectual snobbishness.

Confrontation.   Although you may experience a certain degree of discomfort in using confrontation, it can be a most useful approach. To use it effectively it may be helpful to link it to other strategies. For example, the Adlerians often employ the "stroke-and-spit" strategy. Cultivating a common social interest and tracking the focus of attention will build a joining-type process—positive stroking. In "spitting," the counselor discloses the skillful manuevers of the client by pointing to the specific behavior the client uses to achieve his or her purposes. Here-and-now behavior is the usual focus, with the disclosure being unpleasant enough that the client no longer desires to continue the behavior (Nikelly and O'Connell, 1971). If you "spit in someone's soup" they tend not to want to repeat the behavior. Humor and exaggeration can be used to soften a confronting focus. Such a disarming approach will reduce the likelihood of guarded or defensive behavior: "Let's see if we can make it worse" or "You are very clever; by pretending to be weak, you have become powerful."

IDENTIFYING IRRATIONAL BELIEFS

In your work with clients during career counseling, you may hear statements that Lewis and Gilhousen (1981) refer to as career myths. According to these authors career myths are statements that reflect clients' thoughts about the career development process that are based on underlying irrational beliefs. Here are some typical client statements.

"I am not sure if I want to do this the rest of my life."
"I want to be sure that I don't have to change majors at midyear and lose my credits."
"I think I had better be sure since I am deciding for the rest of my life."
(Lewis and Gilhousen, 1981, p. 297)

The irrational belief underlying such statements is, "I must be absolutely certain before I can act (make a decision, gather information, do anything that requires risk)" (Lewis and Hilhouser, 1981, p. 297). Such thinking creates a paradox. The client must be sure before action can take place, but there is no way the client can be sure unless the client acts first.

With such clients the task is to help them become aware of the irrational beliefs they hold. As they become aware of these beliefs and their effects, you can then begin to introduce alternative, more rational beliefs for consideration. In the case of the above client, a more rational alternative belief might be:

"I may not be sure; however, that does not mean that I cannot do something now. If I act now, I will be gaining information that will be important to me in decisions I will make in the future." (Lewis and Gilhousen, 1981, p. 297)

If your clients are using irrational beliefs to guide their daily living at home, in school, or on the job, it is recommended that you help them become aware of this and deal with it in terms of a chain of events, A-B-C-D-E. To illustrate the use of this procedure, the following case is presented. The case used was adapted by Weinrach from a case originally presented by Ellis (1977).

JOSE: AN OVERVIEW*

Jose is trying to enter the labor force for the first time. He is an 18-year-old high school graduate with a background in automobile mechanics. His native language is Spanish. His oral English is adequate, but his written expression is poor. His other basic skills are also weak. He reported being depressed because he would never be able to get a job and told of having been rejected after his last job interview. This case is presented to demonstrate the applicability of Ellis's (1977, p. 44) Irrational Idea no. 1: I must do well and win the approval of others for my performance or else I will rate as a rotten person.

Activating Experience (A): Performed poorly during job interview and was subsequently not offered the job.

Beliefs (B)

Rational Beliefs (r^B) (wants and desires): I would have liked that job. I don't like getting rejected. Being rejected is a big inconvenience. It was unfortunate that I did so poorly in the interview. I may find getting a job a lot harder than I expected.

Irrational Beliefs (i^B) (demands and commands): It is awful that I got rejected. I can't stand being rejected. Being rejected means that I am a rotten person. I'll never get a job that I want. I will always do poorly on job interviews.

Consequence (Emotional) of Beliefs about Activating Experience (C): Depressed, worthless, rejected, helpless, hopeless.

Disputing or Debating Irrational Beliefs (D) (stated in the form of questions): What is so awful about having not been offered a job? What evidence do I have that I can't stand having been rejected? How does having been rejected from one job interview make me a rotten person? How do I know that I will never get a job that I want? Why must I always do poorly on job interviews?

Effects of Disputing or Debating Irrational Beliefs (E)

Cognitive Effects (c^E): Nothing makes it awful to have been rejected, especially as a lot of people apply for the same job and it is impossible for everybody to get that job; I can stand rejection. This isn't the first time I was turned down, but I don't like the feeling. Being rejected only means that I wasn't offered this particular job and in no way does that make me a rotten person. It is too soon to tell whether or not I'll ever get a job that I like, but being eighteen would suggest that I have time on my side. I'll just have to wait and try some more. I don't have to do poorly on job interviews for the rest of my life. Maybe a little practice will help. I do have some bad traits that seem to come out when I am under stress. But all humans have some bad characteristics. If they didn't, they'd be perfect and no human is perfect.

Emotional Effects (e^E): I am disappointed but not depressed.

Behavioral Effects (b^E): I will go for more job interviews; I will get some lessons from my counselor on how to act during interviews and then practice with my peers and parents. I will register with State Employment and local CETA program for kids my age.

Summary: As a result of RET, Jose ceased making self-deprecatory statements. He also began to see that the situation was not, as he had previously defined it, hopeless. Nor was he helpless. There were things he could do to

---

* S. G. Weinrach, "A Rational-Emotive Approach to Occupational Mental Health," *The Vocational Guidance Quarterly*, 28, no. 3 (1980), 213–14. Reprinted with permission.

improve his chances for a job. Once he felt disappointed and not depressed, he regained the emotional energy to try to find a job again.

IDENTIFYING DISTORTED THINKING

Another way to listen to and understand clients during career counseling is to identify distorted thinking. Distorted thinking involves the use of partial information from which to draw conclusions, faulty perceptions, and inadequate or partial generalizations of information and ideas. A list of fifteen types of distorted thinking and their definitions, as developed by McKay, Davis, and Fanning is given below*:

1. *Filtering:* You take the negative details and magnify them while filtering out all positive aspects of a situation.
2. *Polarized Thinking:* Things are black or white, good or bad. You have to be perfect or you're a failure. There is no middle ground.
3. *Overgeneralization:* You come to a general conclusion based on a single incident or piece of evidence. If something bad happens once you expect it to happen over and over again.
4. *Mind Reading:* Without their saying so, you know what people are feeling and why they act the way they do. In particular, you are able to divine how people are feeling toward you.
5. *Catastrophizing:* You expect disaster. You notice or hear about a problem and start "what ifs": What if tragedy strikes? What if it happens to you?"
6. *Personalization:* Thinking that everything people do or say is some kind of reaction to you. You also compare yourself to others, trying to determine who's smarter, better looking, etc.
7. *Control Fallacies:* If you feel externally controlled, you see yourself as helpless, a victim of fate. The fallacy of internal control has you responsible for the pain and happiness of everyone around you.
8. *Fallacy of Fairness:* You feel resentful because you think you know what's fair but other people won't agree with you.
9. *Blaming:* You hold other people responsible for your pain, or take the other tack and blame yourself for every problem or reversal.
10. *Shoulds:* You have a list of ironclad rules about how you and other people should act. People who break the rules anger you and you feel guilty if you violate the rules.
11. *Emotional Reasoning:* You believe that what you feel must be true—automatically. If you feel stupid and boring, then you must be stupid and boring.
12. *Fallacy of Change:* You expect that other people will change to suit you if you just pressure or cajole them enough. You need to change people because your hopes for happiness seem to depend entirely on them.

* M. McKay, M. Davis, and P. Fanning, *Thoughts and Feelings: The Art of Cognitive Stress Intervention* (Richmond, Calif.: New Harbinger Publications, 1981), p. 26. Reprinted with permission.

13. *Global Labeling:* You generalize one or two qualities into a negative global judgment.
14. *Being Right:* You are continually on trial to prove that your opinions and actions are correct. Being wrong is unthinkable and you will go to any length to demonstrate your rightness.
15. *Heaven's Reward Fallacy:* You expect all your sacrifice and self-denial to pay off, as if there were someone keeping score. You feel bitter when the reward doesn't come.

USING REFLECTIVE JUDGMENT STAGES

Still another way to understand, interpret, and work with client behavior exhibited during career counseling is to focus attention on how clients make judgments about themselves, others, and the world in which they live. A useful model that describes this process in a seven-stage format is outlined by Welfel (1982). Stage progression is on a continuum. At any point one stage may dominate, but adjacent stages also are present to some degree in the person's thinking (Rest, 1979). The seven stages outlined by Welfel are as follows*:

STAGE 1

This first stage is identified by absolutist thinking. Reality is directly knowable and knowledge exists absolutely. Authorities possess absolute knowledge and it is assumed that one's own views ought to correspond with those of authority. Beliefs simply exist and justification of one's beliefs is not seen as necessary because differences in opinion are simply not perceived.

STAGE 2

This stage is also characterized by the belief that knowledge is both certain and possible to obtain but there is a beginning recognition of alternative concepts of reality. The individual has discovered that authorities can disagree but explains these disagreements by dividing authorities into two categories, legitimate and illegitimate. Beliefs simply exist or are justified by reference to the absolute knowledge of a legitimate authority.

STAGE 3

The realization that even legitimate authorities disagree, thereby putting into doubt the certainty of knowledge, leads persons to Stage 3. At Stage 3 absolute knowledge is seen as limited to certain areas (often science) but not possible in other areas. In those uncertain domains, individuals are free to believe anything they choose while awaiting the emergence of the truth. When evidence is used to justify a belief, it is thought of in a quantitative rather than [a] qualitative way; that is, if one accumulates a quantity of infor-

* E. R. Welfel, "The Development of Reflective Judgment: Implications for Career Counseling of College Students," *The Personnel and Guidance Journal,* 61, no. 1 (1982), p. 18. Reprinted with permission.

mation to support a view then that view must be correct. The dissonance of holding unjustified beliefs in the face of environments that ask for justification (such as college campuses) motivates movement to Stage 4.

STAGE 4

The hallmark of Stage 4 is the acknowledgment of uncertainty as a facet of all knowledge. Stage 4 reasoning is that of a practical skeptic. Without certainty or a way to adjudicate between the many possible answers, the individual becomes the source and only judge of his or her personal truths. At this juncture authorities are no longer valued; students frequently comment that the view of any authority is not any more worthwhile than that of anyone else.

STAGE 5

Gradually, a person learns to weigh and evaluate arguments according to a set of rules of evidence. Learning such rules of evidence allows for the emergence of Stage 5 and the capacity to evaluate positions on intellectual problems as stronger or weaker. Beliefs are justified by reference to the rules of inquiry for a particular context: for example, that a simpler scientific theory is preferable to a complex one but knowledge claims cannot extend beyond the rules for that one context. An integrated viewpoint still has not emerged.

STAGE 6

Through the comparison of various perspectives against each other and one's personal experience that typifies Stage 5, the groundwork is prepared for the emergence of Stage 6. At Stage 6 one has moved outside individual frames of reference and now has the capacity to compare and contrast knowledge claims using generalized principles of inquiry. Still, objective knowledge, the ultimate standard against which beliefs can be evaluated, is not yet acknowledged. Beliefs are justified as plausible positions limited to a particular case, time, or person.

STAGE 7

At this final stage fully reflective judgments can be made. With this highest stage comes the recognition that, in spite of the essential uncertainty of knowledge, some judgments about reality are more correct than others. Such judgments can be achieved through the process of critical inquiry and evaluation. The decision rules for evaluation may vary from one domain to another but the assumption that beliefs may be judged as better or worse approximations to reality remains constant. From this perspective, authorities are seen as rational people with extensive knowledge in their disciplines and, thereby, are well worth listening to and learning from. In contrast to Stages 1 and 2, authorities clearly are not viewed as sources of absolute truth anymore.

FOCUSING ON EXCUSES

Another way of understanding, interpreting, and working with client behavior exhibited during career counseling is to examine the concept of excuses. Snyder, Higgins, and Stucky (1983) define excuses as "explanations or actions that lessen the negative implications of an actor's performance, thereby maintaining a positive image for oneself and others" (p. 4).

As the career counseling process unfolds, it may become apparent that your client's behavior is different from what was expected by the client or others. How are such discrepancies explained? Sometimes clients use excuses hoping that they will serve as logical and legitimate reasons for their behavior. Snyder, Higgins, and Stucky (1983) list some common excuses as follows:

LESSENING APPARENT RESPONSIBILITY (I didn't do it.)

Denial
Alibis
Blaming

REFRAMING PERFORMANCES (It's really not so bad.)

Minimization
Justification
Derogation

LESSENING TRANSFORMED RESPONSIBILITY (Yes, but. . . .)

I couldn't help it.
I didn't mean it.
It wasn't really me.

SOME CLOSING THOUGHTS

In this chapter we identified and described nine skills that are useful in working with clients who may be defensive and evasive or may exhibit irrational beliefs and distorted thinking during career counseling. One of our purposes in describing these skills was to highlight their usefulness in understanding and interpreting "how clients construe their experiences" (Blocher, 1980, p. 335) from perspectives not typically used in career counseling. Another purpose was to stress the importance of adding these skills to those you possess already so that the more traditional tools and techniques of career counseling can be used more effectively. As Lewis and Gilhousen (1981, p. 296) point out, "Interests, values, and occupational information are of little consequence if the client cannot put them into realistic perspective." The skills described in this chapter can help you gather, understand, and interpret client information and behavior and can help clients put such information and behavior into "realistic perspective."

REFERENCES

BANDLER, R., and GRINDER, J., *Frogs into Princes*. Moab, Utah: Real People Press, 1979.
——, ——, and SATIR, V., *Changing with Families*. Palo Alto, Calif.: Science and Behavior Books, 1976.
BLOCHER, D. H., "Some Implications of Recent Research in Social and Developmental Psychology for Counseling Practice," *The Personnel and Guidance Journal*, 58, no. 5 (1980), 334–36.
BOLLES, R. N., *What Color is Your Parachute?* Berkeley, Calif.: Ten Speed Press, 1985.
ELLIS, A., *How to Live With and Without Anger*. Pleasantville, N.Y.: Reader's Digest Press, 1977.
GORDON, D., *Therapeutic Metaphors*. Cupertino, Calif.: Meta Publications, 1978.
HARMAN, R. L., and O'NEILL, C., "Neuro Linguistic Programming for Counselors," *The Personnel and Guidance Journal*, 59, no. 7 (1981), 449–53.
LEWIS, R. A., and GILHOUSEN, M. R., "Myths of Career Development: A Cognitive Approach to Vocational Counseling," *The Personnel and Guidance Journal*, 59, no. 5, (1981), 296–99.
LOW, A., *Mental Health Through Will Training* (14th ed.). Boston: Christopher Publishing, 1966.
McKAY, M., DAVIS, M., and FANNING, P., *Thoughts and Feelings: The Art of Cognitive Stress Intervention*. Richmond, Calif.: New Harbinger Publications, 1981.
NIKELLY, A. G., and O'CONNELL, W. E., "Action-Oriented Methods," in *Techniques For Behavior Change*, ed. A. G. Nikelly. Springfield, Ill.: Charles C Thomas, 1971.
RATH, G. J., and STOYANOFF, K. S., "Understanding and Improving Communication Effectiveness," in *The 1982 Annual for Facilitators, Trainers, and Consultants*, eds. J. William Pfeiffer and Leonard D. Goodstein, pp. 166–73. San Diego, Calif: University Associates, 1982.
REST, J., *Development in Judging Moral Issues*. Minneapolis: University of Minnesota Press, 1979.
SNYDER, C. R., HIGGINS, R. L., and STUCKY, R. J., *Excuses: Masquerades in Search of Grace*. New York: John Wiley, 1983.
SHULMAN, B. H., and MOSAK, H. H., "Various Purposes of Symptoms," *Journal of Individual Psychology*, 23, no. 1, (1967), 79–87.
WEINRACH, S. G., "A Rational-Emotive Approach to Occupational Mental Health," *The Vocational Guidance Quarterly*, 28, no. 3 (1980), 208–13.
WELFEL, E. R., "The Development of Reflective Judgment: Implications for Career Counseling of College Students," *The Personnel and Guidance Journal*, 61, no. 1 (1982), 17–21.

CHAPTER 2

Identifying
and Analyzing Life
Career Themes

*People look at the world and develop constructs which organize
and systematize events, people, and the environmental context.
Constructs are hypotheses which the person has used to test some
idea or behavior on the world and found in some way effective.
Constructs, then, are our ideas and representations of the
world—in effect, our worldview. (Ivey and Simek-Downing,
1980, p. 137)*

In the first phase of the career counseling framework
presented in the Introduction (client goal or problem identification, clarification, and specification) major emphasis is placed on understanding and
interpreting client self- and environmental information and the behavior
clients exhibit. Why is this emphasis important in career counseling?
Blocher (1980, p. 335) points out that "literally, what clients say to themselves may be the crucial mediating processes in their lives." We would add
to Blocher's statement the following: What clients say to themselves *about
themselves, others, and the world in which they live and the language they choose to
represent these views* may be the crucial mediating process in their lives. Kelly
(1955) describes this phenomenon in terms of individuals looking at the
world through self-created transparent patterns or templates in order to
make sense out of it. He uses the phrase "personal constructs" to describe
these patterns and states that personal constructs are ways of construing
the world. Bandler and Grinder (1975) point out from another perspective
the need for counselors to pay attention to clients' action, sensory, and
metaphoric language patterns to understand how clients represent their
worlds. Gerber (1983) suggests that the language people use represents
their underlying conceptual schemata, and, in turn, their conceptual schemata determine their behavior.

One way to understand client information and behavior is to focus
attention on the constructs, schemata, or *life career themes*, as we call them,

that clients use to understand themselves, others, and their worlds. What concepts do they use? What are the nature and extent of the vocabulary they use to express these concepts? Is their vocabulary fully developed? Is it limited? Is it based on stereotypes? Does it contain distortions?

As an understanding of client information and behavior begins to emerge, the tasks of interpretation also begin. How do you and your clients interpret this information and behavior? What diagnoses flow from these interpretations?

It is our contention that your skills in understanding and interpreting client information and behavior in career counseling can be expanded and extended by using the concept of life career theme identification and analysis. To use the concept effectively requires in-depth knowledge of as many models as possible that explain human behavior. Such knowledge provides the clues, concepts, and vocabulary to help you see, understand, and interpret client information and behavior in terms of life career themes from a variety of perspectives. What was seemingly unexplainable information or behavior becomes explainable because a particular model gives you a way to see, understand, and explain it.

To help you expand and extend your skills to see, understand, and interpret client information and behavior, Chapter 2 presents a definition of life career themes, followed by a description of the process of life career theme identification and analysis. A structure (life roles) to provide a specific focus for the life career theme identification and analysis process is also presented. Finally, Chapter 2 presents a number of models of human behavior that can provide you and your clients with a variety of useful ways to see, express, and describe life career themes. These models are introduced primarily to help you to understand and interpret client information and behavior in terms of life career themes as a basis for forming diagnoses and then selecting and using intervention strategies to help clients reach their goals and solve their problems. The focus is on the cues and language these models can supply to help you identify and analyze life career themes.

WHAT ARE LIFE CAREER THEMES?
HOW DO WE IDENTIFY AND ANALYZE THEM?

Life career themes are words that people use to express their ideas, values, attitudes, and beliefs about themselves (*I am* statements), about others (*others are* statements), and about the world (*life is* statements). An understanding of themes is important because they provide us with ways to understand the thought processes of our clients. They help us picture our clients' representational systems, and they help us gain insight into our clients' behavior.

Life career theme identification and analysis require a structure to guide the process. The structure we recommend is life roles, in particular, worker, learner, and personal roles. Life roles are used because they can provide a direct and realistic way to organize life career themes that directly relate to clients and the worlds in which they live and work.

Models of human behavior offer ways to describe human and environmental characteristics. They supply the language with which to phrase client life career themes. We suggest the following models because they can be easily linked to the life role structure.

LIFE ROLE	MODELS
Worker	Data-ideas-people-things
	Vocational personalities and work
	environments
	Skills identification
Learner	Learner styles
	Learning styles
Personal	Life-style
	Hemispheric functioning

Each model presents a particular way of looking at, understanding, interpreting, and expressing client behavior. To carry out theme identification and analysis, the counselor's task is to take the images formed about clients from the samples of their behavior obtained during career counseling and to translate these images into the language of models. The language of the models becomes the language used to express the life career themes that have been identified.

Steps Involved

The first step in life career theme identification and analysis occurs during the first phase of the career counseling process. It occurs during the time when you are gathering client self- and environmental information. It may involve the use of standardized instruments such as the Strong-Campbell Interest Inventory, structured materials such as card sorts, or structured interviews such as the life career assessment (see Chapter 3). From the information gathered from these and other sources images are formed about what the client is like.

The next step involves translating the images you have formed into the language of one or more of the models you may be using. In effect, you look at the images formed through the eyes of the model or models and interpret what you see in their language. For example, if you are using Holland's classification system (1985) as your model, you could use one or more of the personality types he describes as possible descriptors of the client images you have formed. The developers of the Strong-Campbell

Interest Inventory did this when they cast part of the interpretation of the inventory in the Holland personality types language.

The last step in theme analysis is developing an in-your-mind profile of the themes you have derived from the client images you have formed. One way to do this is to visualize the client themes you have identified as brief newspaper articles about them complete with headlines. In your mind you write the article describing your client in terms of the themes and then summarize the key themes as boldface news headlines.

Some Points to Remember in Theme Analysis

Some career counseling approaches emphasize the gathering of all the facts before attempting to explain client behavior. We believe that this is not always effective or efficient because when you are working with clients you will be dealing with their unique streams of behavior and their private logic (Nikelly, 1971). We recommend that instead of waiting to explain and interpret client themes until all of the information about them is gathered, you begin immediately in the career counseling process to form hypotheses about your clients' unique combinations of themes and their resulting behavior. As the counseling process unfolds, you will accept or reject hypotheses in part or totally on a continuing basis. Rather than trying to impose psychological certainties after all the information is in, the use of hypotheses invites you to get on with the task of understanding the life career themes your clients may be using, to test out your understanding of them with your clients, and to profit from mistaken or divergent views.

Sometimes in the career counseling process you will note life career theme inconsistencies in clients. These often are difficult to understand. A possible way to resolve inconsistent and contradictory themes is to use a technique called two points in a line (Dreikurs, 1966). This technique suggests that inconsistencies and contradictions in themes are simply a matter of our inability to grasp the logic that binds them into a coherent whole. If you are able to connect two divergent themes, it may be possible to understand your clients' behavior in a wide range of situations. As in geometry, the location of a line can be determined by two points. The key to resolving apparent inconsistencies and contradictions is to find the string that links the points together. For example, some individuals who are aware of their weaknesses counter those weaknesses through compensation. Thus you may observe their more primitive behavior sometimes and their compensating behavior at other times. For example, a client may exhibit primitive behavior in a stressful situation. The fact that clients are using compensation is, in itself, a useful piece of information that will help you understand them better.

It is important to keep in mind that you need to avoid premature and absolute categorization of clients based on the themes you identify. Life career theme analysis is not a technique to help you gather perceptions about clients and then label them for all time on the basis of these perceptions. Instead, life career theme analysis is a technique that serves as a point of departure for exploration and decision making. As themes are identified they serve as discussion points to aid both you and your clients to better understand who they are, where they may be going, and what concerns may be present.

Finally, as you are using life career theme analysis as a part of career counseling, keep in mind that you can look at each bit of information about your clients in a number of ways. What does it mean as a sample? Is this a common or unusual occurrence? With what does the information correlate? Does it often follow or precede certain events? Is it a sign of an underlying condition? What does it symbolize?

MODEL EXPLANATIONS

As we stated previously, you will need to select models of human behavior to supply the appropriate language to help you describe the life career themes you and your clients identify. We suggest a structure that uses the worker, learner, and personal life roles and one or more models to supply the perspective and the language to express the identified themes. What follows are brief explanations of these models and some examples of how to apply them to life career theme analysis.

Worker Role

Data-Ideas-People-Things—Prediger. The most widely used and influential occupational classification system is the *Dictionary of Occupational Titles* published by the U.S. Department of Labor (1977). Prediger (1976) extended the data-people-things worker function ratings to include ideas. He defined these as follows:

> *Data* (facts, records, files, numbers; systematic procedures for facilitating goods/services consumption by people). Data tasks involve impersonal processes, such as recording, verifying, transmitting, and organizing facts or data representing goods and services. Purchasing agents, accountants, and air traffic controllers work mainly with data.
>
> *Ideas* (abstractions, theories, knowledge, insights, and new ways of expressing something, for example, with words, equations, or music). Ideas tasks involve intrapersonal processes, such as creating, discovering, interpreting, and synthesizing abstractions or implementing applications of abstractions. Scientists, musicians, and philosophers work mainly with ideas.
>
> *People.* People tasks involve interpersonal processes, such as helping, serving, persuading, entertaining, motivating, and directing—in general, producing a

change in human behavior. Teachers, salespersons, and nurses work mainly with people.

Things (machines, mechanisms, materials, tools, physical and biological processes). Things tasks involve nonpersonal processes, such as producing, transporting, servicing, and repairing. Bricklayers, farmers, and engineers work mainly with things. (Prediger, 1976, p. 202)

Prediger suggests that the two work-task dimensions of data versus ideas and things versus people constitute the primary dimensions for occupations and interests. He overlayed Holland's hexagonal model of occupational personality types on these two dimensions and then developed an occupational mapping procedure known as the World-of-Work Map. (For more information concerning the development and application of this procedure, see "Mapping Occupations and Interest: A Graphic Aid for Vocational Guidance and Research" [Prediger, 1981].)

Our purpose in presenting this model is to focus on its application to the process of life career theme analysis. Of particular interest is the language it can supply to help describe the images you form about clients during the career counseling process. As you will see when you read Prediger's article, Holland's occupational classification system as well as a number of interest inventories can be integrated into his data-ideas-people-things work task dimensions.

The following are some sample applications of theme analysis using the language of Prediger's work-task approach.

TYPICAL CLIENT DIALOGUE	COMPONENT DESCRIPTORS	THEME STATEMENTS
"People always seem to come to me for advice." "I like being around young people . . . they are so stimulating."	*People:* Instruct—persuade, help to perform, ability to communicate, serve others	Enjoys selling others . . . Wants to teach others . . . Likes counseling and caring for others
"Being an office manager would be challenging." "I fell I have some expertise that would be of value to others."	*People:* Manage—supervise, consult, act as mentor, leadership	Aspires to be a consultant in . . . Wants others to follow one's lead Finds directing others to accomplish tasks rewarding
"It is important to have everything organized and in order." "They say I'm good with numbers."	*Data:* Abstract—numerical skills, symbols and ideas, information/data collection, data entry technology skills	Likes to manipulate financial data Intrigued by computer technology Prefers to organize information for budgets

"I like to make copies of original artwork." "Monogramming clothing is fun."	*Data:* Creative—design reproduction, craft skills, composition, applied arts	Can duplicate originals Products show attention to detail Can be counted on to complete tasks
"It feels good to be active and perspire." "Being outdoors makes me high."	*Things:* Physical—recreational skills, agriculture/outdoor stamina/strengths for jobs, performance oriented	Can show you how to do things Possesses physical skills for heavy work Contact with nature spurs activity
"I can repair anything that has moving parts." "I lose track of time when I am remodeling my car."	*Ideas:* Artistic—entertainment interests, performing arts (music, acting, etc.), literary creative design	Is a sensitive performer and artist Has the ability to express feelings in writing Has an original way of doing things
"I would like to devote my life to the study of the adrenal gland." "Each answer leads to another question."	*Ideas:* Investigative—social science, medical science, natural science, applied technology	Likes to construct theories to explain world conditions Constantly comparing and contrasting ideas Has the capacity to research and publish

Vocational Personality and Work Environments—Holland. Holland's occupational classification system categorizes personalities and environments into six model types as follows*:

REALISTIC PERSONALITY AND ENVIRONMENT

Persons with a predominantly realistic personality tend to be more oriented to the present and to dealing with the concrete rather than the abstract. They are people who believe they have athletic or mechanical ability and prefer to work in the outdoors with their hands, tools, machines, plants, or animals rather than with people. They prefer the straightforward, measurable, and tried-and-true rather than the unknown and unpredictable. They often exhibit a straightforward stick-to-itiveness and sense of maturity.

The environment is one that encourages and rewards success in the use of one's hands and in the manipulation of things. It is a world of the tangible and predictable, which rewards with and values money, possessions, and power.

---

* Adapted from John L. Holland, *Making Vocational Choices: A Theory of Vocational Personalities and Work Environments,* 2nd ed. (Englewood Cliffs, N.J.: Prentice-Hall, 1985), pp. 19–23, 36–40. Used with permission.

INVESTIGATIVE PERSONALITY AND ENVIRONMENT

Persons with a predominantly investigative personality tend to be more oriented to the abstract and problem solving. They like to solve problems that require thinking, especially involving the scientific, technical, and mathematical. They tend not to be particularly socially oriented and prefer academic and scientific success. They value the intellect and believe it is the tool with which to deal with the world.

The environment is one that encourages and rewards success in the use of the intellect and in the manipulation of the abstract. It is a world of observing, investigating, and theorizing, and it values and rewards with status and recognition.

ARTISTIC PERSONALITY AND ENVIRONMENT

Persons with a predominantly artistic personality tend to be more oriented to the imaginative and creative, using feelings as a guide to whether something is right. They have, or believe they have, artistic, innovative, or intuitive abilities and prefer to avoid structured work settings and conformity. They value the aesthetic and often prefer to relate to the world through the products of their work such as paintings, plays, and music.

The environment is one that encourages and rewards the display of the above-mentioned values. It is a world of the abstract, aesthetic, and original. It rewards with recognition, status, and increasing freedom to create in one's own way.

SOCIAL PERSONALITY AND ENVIRONMENT

Persons with a predominantly social personality tend to be more oriented to the problems and growth of people and interpersonal relationships. They like to work with people directly, and are good with words. They like to inform, teach, help, and train others. They often are academically oriented. However, they tend toward the impulsive and intuitive rather than the methodical and scientific.

The environment is one that encourages and rewards success in the above-mentioned values and tends to promote social activities. It is a world of people and relationships that is often changing, and it values social skills and the ability to promote change in others. It tends to reward with recognition and approval from peers and those being taught and helped.

ENTERPRISING PERSONALITY AND ENVIRONMENT

Persons with a predominantly enterprising personality tend to be more oriented to the overcoming of political and economic challenges. They are, or believe they are, good at talking and using words to persuade, influence, and manage for organizational or economic goals. They tend to be more assertive and dominating than other types. They often value and seek out new challenges and tend to be self-confident as well as social, although this is often at a surface level.

The environment is one that encourages and rewards success in the above. It is a world of continual new challenges to be overcome, valuing and rewarding power, status, and money.

CONVENTIONAL PERSONALITY AND ENVIRONMENT

Persons with a predominantly conventional personality tend to be more conforming and conventional, preferring the structured and predictable. They like to work with data, and have, or believe they have, clerical or numerical ability. They prefer to follow others' directions and carry out activities in detail. They tend to value the neat and the orderly and prefer not to be responsible for the intangible and unpredictable.

The environment is one that encourages and rewards exacting management of data and details. It is a world of facts that is practical and organized, where dependability and attention to detail are rewarded. Rewards tend to be in the area of economic success and status involving material possessions and recognition of superiors and peers.

Holland's theory states that by comparing a person's attributes to each model type, we can determine which type the individual resembles most. Since individuals resemble more than one type, we also determine to what extent they resemble the other types. The three types that the individual most resembles describes that person's code. For example, a person who is a counselor might have the code SAE, which indicates that this person resembles the social type most and the artistic and the enterprising types to a lesser degree,

The codes are most easily understood using Holland's hexagonal model. The hexagon with the first letter of each type looks like this.

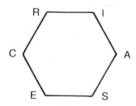

Types that are adjacent to each other on the hexagon are more similar than the types directly across from each other. S is more similar to A and E than it is to R. Codes consisting of closely related types occur more frequently than those that do not. For example, codes such as ESC and RIC occur more frequently than codes such as CSI and IES.

The language used by Holland to describe personality types and environments is very useful in translating the images of clients into theme statements. It can be easily related to how clients think and talk about themselves. You also will find that Holland's descriptions are used in a number of interest inventories as a means of interpreting the results to clients.

Skills Identification—Bolles.   In his book *The Three Boxes of Life* Bolles (1981) divides skills into three major categories: self-management skills, functional/transferable skills, and work-content skills. Bolles defines self-management skills as the ones a person would use to get along with others and to relate to authority, time, space, and the material world. Functional/ transferable skills describe how people act on information, people, and things. These skills are transferable, as the title suggests. Work-content skills focus on mastering vocabulary, work-related techniques and procedures, and subject matter.

The language used to describe the skills people have in all three categories is useful in theme analysis. Bolles and Zenoff state that skills in the functional/transferable category are the most difficult to identify and yet potentially the most important. They developed a technique, called The Quick Job-Hunting Map, to help people identify those skills (Bolles and Zenoff, 1977, pp. 9–15) in which they present the following subcategories of functional/transferable skills:

A. Using my hands
B. Using my body
C. Using words
D. Using my senses
E. Using numbers
F. Using intuition
G. Using analytical thinking or logic
H. Using originality or creativity
I. Using helpfulness
J. Using artistic abilities
K. Using leadership, being up front
L. Using follow-through

In each of the subcategories a number of specific skills are identified, and examples of where these skills may be used are provided. The language used to describe the skills and the examples provided can be used by you and your clients to help identify and describe skills. The language used provides the nucleus around which life career themes can be grouped. If you are not familiar with skill identification as described by Bolles and Zenoff, you may wish to read *What Color is Your Parachute* (Bolles, 1985).

Combining Worker Role Models

The models that we have suggested to help you identify and describe client themes related to the worker role can be used separately or in various combinations. Prediger, for example, combined the occupational classification system of Holland with data-ideas-people-things in the development of his world of work map. As another example, we combined the personality types from Holland's occupational classification system with the skill identification process of Bolles to provide an additional way of identifying and describing client themes.

All of the examples that follow use the same format. First, the personality type is described. Then examples of functional/transferable skills associated with that type are listed. A listing of sample theme descriptors is also provided.

ARTISTIC

The artistic personality has an interest in creative expression of feelings or ideas. Complex mental skills are used to create new knowledge or new ways of applying what is already known. This includes different problems or designing projects and methods; using new ways to express ideas, feelings, and moods; and using imagination to create ideas and moods. Examples and prior experiences might include handicrafts, photography, art, painting, decorating, playing in a band, or singing in a choir.

Functional/Transferable Skills

Skill	Specific Operations
1. Using originality/creativity	1. Imagining, inventing, designing; improvising, adapting, experimenting
2. Using artistic ability	2. Composing, playing music, singing; shaping materials, creating shapes or faces, using colors; showing feelings and thoughts through body, face, or voice, using words expressively.
3. Using intuition	3. Showing foresight, acting on gut reactions, quickly sizing up a situation.

Career Theme

Dislikes routine; dislikes supervision; expressive; intuitive, original; adventurous, likes novelty, change, variety; attention-getting; impulsive; independent, nonconforming; spontaneous; abstract thinking.

SOCIAL

The social personality has an interest in helping individuals with their mental, spiritual, social, physical, or occupational concerns. This interest can be satisfied through jobs in which maintaining or improving the physical, mental, emotional, or spiritual well-being of others is important. Speaking and listening well, communicating simple ideas, and having direct contact with the people being helped are also important. Examples and prior experiences might include being a disc jockey, public speaking, writing for the school paper, and organizing a basketball game.

Functional/Transferable Skills

Skill	Specific Operations
1. Using words	1. Reading, copying, editing, writing, teaching, training, memorizing
2. Using helpfulness	2. Drawing out people, motivating, counseling; appreciating, sharing credit, raising others' self-esteem

Career Theme

Social contact; adaptable; interested; cooperative; kind; likes friends to approach; insightful; generous; sociable; guiding; understanding; popular; idealistic; convincing; friendly; expressive; committed.

ENTERPRISING

The enterprising personality has an interest in influencing others and enjoys the challenge and responsibility of leadership. Activities involved may include setting up business contacts to buy, sell, talk, listen, promote, and bargain; gathering, exchanging, or presenting ideas and facts about products or services; leading, planning, controlling, or managing the work or others and as a result gaining prestige, recognition, or appreciation from others. Examples and prior experiences might include managing a paper route, selling candy or tickets, Jr. Achievement, being a Candy Striper, babysitting, or starting a money-making project.

Educational/Transferable Skills

Skill	Specific Operations
1. Using leadership	1. Starting new tasks, ideas, taking the first move; organizing, leading, making decisions; taking risks, performing, selling, promoting, persuading

Career Theme

Dislikes routine; adaptable; adventurous; dislikes supervision; seeks reward and recognition; ambitious; energetic; independent; sociable; persuasive; manipulating; aggressive; competitive; impulsive; assertive; optimistic; self-confident.

CONVENTIONAL

The conventional personality is organized to get the most work done in the least amount of time. Setting up assignments and methods in advance and repeating the same task many times may be involved. These tasks can usually be done in a short time. Activities involved may be those requiring accuracy and attention to details. Examples might include record keeping, billing, filing, or recording, keeping a checkbook, developing a budget, and savings.

Functional/Transferable Skills

Skill	Specific Operations
1. Using numbers	1. Taking inventory, counting, calculating; keeping financial records, managing money; number memory
2. Using follow-through	2. Following through on plans, instructions, attending to detail; classifying, recording, filing

Career Theme

Likes details; likes to complete tasks; careful; persistent; systemic-structured; efficient; conforming; practical; conservative; orderly; inhibited; conscientious.

REALISTIC

The realistic personality uses physical skills to work on or make products. This interest can be satisfied in a variety of work ranging from routine to complex jobs. It may involve using physical skills to work on or make products. It also may involve dealing directly with things. Often tools, machines, or measuring devices are used to make or change a product or build, repair, alter, or restore products. Complex tasks are involved such as adjusting and controlling things or using knowledge and reasoning skills to make judgments and decisions. Examples and prior experiences might include repairing a bicycle, mowing lawns, typing, highly skilled crafts, using a printing press.

Functional/Transferable Skills

Skill	Specific Operations
1. Using hands	1. Assembling, constructing, building, operating tools, machinery or equipment; showing finger dexterity, precision handling, and repairing
2. Using body	2. Physical activity, muscular coordination, outdoor activities

Career Theme

Likes detail; likes to complete tasks; systematic-structured; efficient; confident; handles objects; works with tools; works with machines; conforming; precision work; pratical; methodical; materialistic; frank; honest; humble; natural; persistent; modest; shy; stable; thrifty.

INVESTIGATIVE

The investigative personality has an interest in researching and collecting data about the natural world and applying them to problems in medical, life, or physical sciences. This interest may be satisfied by working with the knowledge and processes involved in the sciences. Conducting research and analyzing, evaluating, explaining, and recording scientific information as well as using scientific or technical methods, instruments, and equipment in work are involved. Planning, scheduling, processing, controlling, directing, and evaluating data and things also are involved. There may be contact with people, but dealing with people is not important to the work. Examples and prior experiences might include computer work, operating complex machines, assisting in a laboratory, finding the location of an unfamiliar street, tracing down a short in electrical wiring, finding the ingredients to a special recipe, comparative shopping, examining a cut or bruise.

Functional/Transferable Skills

Skill	Specific Operations
1. Using analytical thinking or logic	1. Researching, information gathering, analyzing; organizing, diagnosing, putting things in order, comparing, testing, evaluation
2. Using senses	2. Observing, inspecting, examining; diagnosing, showing attention to detail

Career Theme

Analytical; efficient; cautious; likes to investigate; curious; methodical; seeks to understand; thinks to solve problems; precision work; independent; modest; seeks to organize; reserved.

Learner Role

Learner Styles—Kolb. In the early 1970s Kolb developed a model to explain learning style that is based on how we perceive and process. The model is represented by continuums that go from concrete experience to abstract conceptualization (perception) and from active experimentation to reflective observation (process). This model is expressed graphically as follows:

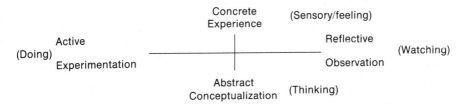

Kolb believes that one's dominant learning style is a result of heredity, past life experiences, and the demands of the present environment, such as family, school, or job. Day-by-day decision making involves the use of the learning modes depicted above. The pressure and habit of such decision making shape the learning process into one of four general patterns or learning styles: the converger, the diverger, the assimilator, and the accommodator. Kolb (1976) developed a self-descriptive inventory called the Learning Style Inventory (LSI) to measure these learning styles. The following is a summary of the characteristics of these types.*

CONVERGER

Convergers' dominant learning abilities are abstract conceptualization (AC) and active experimentation (AE). Their greatest strength lies in the practical application of ideas. The convergers seem to do best in those situations, such as conventional intelligence tests, where there is a single correct answer or solution to a question or problem. Their knowledge is organized in such a way that, through hypothetical-deductive reasoning, they can focus on specific problems. Convergers are relatively unemotional, preferring to deal with things rather than people. They tend to have narrow interests, and often choose to specialize in the physical sciences. This learning style is characteristic of many engineers.

DIVERGER

The divergers have the opposite learning strengths of the convergers. They are best at concrete experience (CE) and reflective observation (RO). Their greatest strength lies in their imaginative ability. They excel in the ability to view concrete situations from many perspectives and to organize many relationships into a meaningful gestalt. Persons of this type perform better in situations that call for the generation of ideas, such as in a brainstorming idea session. Divergers are interested in people and tend to be imaginative and emotional. They have broad cultural interests and tend to specialize in the arts. This style is characteristic of persons with humanities and liberal arts backgrounds. Counselors, organization development consultants, and personnel managers often have this learning style.

ASSIMILATOR

The assimilators' dominant learning abilities are abstract conceptualization (AC) and reflective observation (RO). Their greatest strength lies in their ability to create theoretical models. They excel in inductive reasoning; in assimilating disparate observations into an integrated explanation. They are less interested in people and more concerned about abstract concepts, but they are not particularly concerned with the practical use of theories. It is more important that the theory be logically sound and precise. As a result, this learning style is more characteristic of the basic sciences and mathematics

---

* Adapted from David A. Kolb, *Experiential Learning: Experience as the Source of Learning and Development* (Englewood Cliffs, N.J.: Prentice-Hall, 1984), pp. 77–78. Used with permission.

than the applied sciences. In organizations, this learning style is found most often, in persons who work in the research and planning departments.

ACCOMMODATOR

The accommodators have the opposite strengths of assimilators. They are best at concrete experience (CE) and active experimentation (AE). Their greatest strength lies in doing things; in carrying out plans and experiments and involving themselves in new experiences. Accommodators are more likely to be risk takers than people with the other three learning styles. They tend to excel in those situations in which they must adapt to specific immediate circumstances. In situations where the theory or plans do not fit the facts, they will most likely discard the plan or theory. (The opposite type, the assimilator, would be more likely to disregard or reexamine the facts.) They tend to solve problems in an intuitive, trial-and-error manner relying heavily on other people for information rather than their own analytic abililty. Accommodators are at ease with people but are sometimes seen as impatient and pushy. Their educational background is often in technical and practical fields such as business. In organizations people with this learning style are found in action-oriented jobs, such as marketing or sales.

These learning styles are placed in the model presented previously as follows:

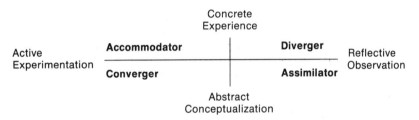

Wolfe and Kolb (1980) researched the relationship between individual learning styles and the types of occupations people choose. Here are a few examples of what they found. Elementary education majors and teachers are characterized by a high concrete experience orientation. Interest in working with children is associated with a concrete orientation. Alcoholism counselors/therapists and human services workers also show a very high concrete experience orientation and very high reflective observation scores. Organizational development specialists have a similar but less pronounced pattern, particularly on the active-to-reflective scale. Medical school students show an interesting change from the first to fourth years. First-year students made up the highest scoring sample on abstract conceptualization, probably because of the abstract nature of medical school selection procedures. In fourth-year students, however, this changes markedly toward active experimentation. Industrial salesmen have the highest score of any group on active experimentation (the doing dimension), and computer programmers show the high abstract orientation one would predict for a very symbol-oriented job. The patterns of scores taken collectively across all the different groups suggest that learning style scores show sufficient variabililty across different populations to be useful in assessing the learning styles that characterize occupations and groups.

Learning Styles—Canfield. Canfield (1977) developed an instrument based on a learning styles model to measure some of the affective variables that seem to affect learning and that contribute to satisfactory and effective adjustment to the teaching-learning situation. The instrument is called the Learning Styles Inventory. Our purpose in presenting this model is the same as for the other models. The language of this model, which has a learner-instructional orientation, can be applied to the images you form of your clients to help turn these images into themes.

Brief descriptions of the four affective variables that Canfield (1977) has identified as constituting learning styles are presented below*:

Conditions. Canfield chose to measure four sources of motivation that are present in the learning situation. These four areas of motivation are affiliation, structure, achievement, and eminence.

> *Affiliation* concerns the desire to have warm, friendly, supportive relations with other people. On the LSI this area is further broken down into two areas.
> *Peer-affiliation* measures a preference for working in student teams, having student friends, and having good relations with other students. This interest in associations with peers is not based on a need for a competitive comparing of performance, but a need for mutually supportive and friendly relationships.
> *Instructor-affiliation* examines the extent to which the student values knowing the instructor personally, having a mutual understanding, and liking one another.
> *Structure* concerns the desire for logical, orderly, well-defined, and clear study plans. Two LSI scales assess this area.
> *Organization* looks at the student's preference for coursework that is logically and clearly organized, meaningful assignments, and planned sequences of activities. Students with a high preference in this area want to know what the events are going to be, but also why they are in the order they are occurring. They want to know how specific assignments relate to each other and to the objectives of the course.
> *Detail* measures a preference for specific information on assignments, requirements, procedures, rules, and so on. The student with a high preference for detail wants precise and specific information about what is to be done, how to do it, when it is due, and how it will be evaluated.
> *Achievement* concerns preferences for independent action, pursuit of one's own interests, and setting one's own goals in light of a self-assessment of abilities. Two scales contribute to this area.

---

* Adapted from A. A. Canfield, *Learning Style Inventory* (Plymouth, Mich.: Humanics, Inc., 1977), pp. 6–8. Used with permission.

Goal setting determines the student's preference for setting his or her goals, using feedback to modify goals or procedures, and making decisions on goals. These students desire the chance to examine their own capabilities and interests and then select their own objectives.

Independence measures the desire to work alone and independently, determine one's own study plan, and do things for one's self. Students scoring high in this area desire considerable personal freedom to establish goals and the ways and means to achieve them.

Eminence deals with preferences for comparing oneself to others, competing for recognition as well as being in a controlled situation, and dealing with authority. There are two scales in this area.

Competition assesses the student's wish to compare one's own work with that of others, and to know how well one is doing in relation to others.

Authority examines the student's desire for a classroom in which discipline and order are maintained. It also looks at the desire for knowledgeable instructors. Students scoring high on this scale tend to want a well-controlled formal learning environment and teachers who maintain order and provide the right answers.

Content. There is considerable evidence indicating that individuals seem to perform best when they are studying material in which they are highly interested. Consequently, the LSI contains items that assess the individual's level of interest in four areas: numerical-mathematical, qualitative-verbal, inanimate-manipulative, and people-interactive.

Numeric concerns preferences for working with numbers and logic, computing, and solving mathematical problems.

Qualitative measures preferences for working with words or language, writing, editing, and talking.

Inanimate examines preferences for working with things, as in building, repairing, designing, or operating.

People reveals preferences for working with people, as in interviewing, counseling, selling, and helping. This contact with people may not always be for the purpose of helping, guiding, or supporting others.

Mode. Because it has been found that some people learn more efficiently through one of their sensory systems than another, the LSI contains items that assess the student's preference for modes for receiving information. These are listening or auditory, reading, iconic (pictures, graphs), and direct experience (touching, manipulating).

Listening indicates a preference for gaining and receiving information auditorially, as in hearing speeches, lectures, and tapes.

Reading examines a preference for receiving information through the written word, as in reading texts, pamphlets, and magazines.

Iconic measures a preference for obtaining information by means of viewing illustrations, movies, slides, pictures, and graphs.

Direct experience determines a preference for learning information through direct experience, such as handling or performing in shop, laboratory, field trips, and practice exercises.

Expectation. Canfield was impressed by research that demonstrated the importance of expectations in an individual's chances of success. Included on the LSI are items that generate data used to figure the student's expectancy score, which provides information regarding to what degree the student expects to succeed.

> *Outstanding or superior* indicates an expectation to excel, to perform in the top 10% of the class.
>
> *Above average or good* indicates a belief that the student will perform above average, ranking in the top 25% to 30% of the class.
>
> *Average or satisfactory* indicates the student's expectation to perform adequate work in the class, ranking in the middle 50%.
>
> *Below average or unsatisfactory* measures the student's expectation to perform poorly or to fail, ranking in the lower half of the class.
>
> *Expectancy Score* is a single score, computed from the scores on the previous four scales, that gives an overall measure of the student's expectations for success.

Canfield's Learning Styles Inventory identifies individual's preferences for conditions, content, mode, and expectancy. Cafferty (1980), in a paper presented at the 1980 American Vocational Association Convention in New Orleans, analyzed Canfield's Learning Styles Inventory and showed the relationship between learning and work environments. Parts of her paper are reprinted here.* Our purpose in doing so is to point out how the language of learning styles as applied to the learner role and the worker role can become the language you can use to describe client life career themes you have identified during career counseling.

"We can assess individuals' preferences for work environments by using Learning Styles Inventories. While, at the present time, these inventories are intended for use in learning environments, many of the characteristics people prefer in the learning environments correspond to similar characteristics in work environments. There are several Learning Styles Inventories available, but for the purpose of this paper, I have selected Canfield's Learning Styles Inventory (1977) to present an analysis.

"This inventory identifies individuals' preferences for conditions, content, mode and expectancy. The group of elements under conditions can greatly assist individuals in identifying those preferences important in the work environment. These include a preference for working with peers or working alone, a preference for organization, attention to detail, know-

---

* Elsie Cafferty, "Learning Style as a Tool in Career Guidance." Paper presented at the American Vocational Association Convention, December 6, 1980. Reprinted with permission.

ing the instructor, and a preference for authority. Through this assessment, individuals will identify which of these conditions are more highly preferred and which have a lower preference. If individuals prefer to work with peers, have good relations with the students, and have student friends, then those jobs in which they work with others the majority of the time would be more satisfying.

"Good relations on the job being important, individuals would tend to work toward building rapport with fellow employees and develop a teamwork approach toward the tasks to be accomplished. Dissatisfaction would probably result if they were working with those to whom this quality was not important. On the other hand, if persons prefer to work alone, then those jobs where the majority of the work is performed independently would be more desirable. When working where teamwork is important, these kinds of persons tend to go ahead and do their own thing with little regard for the togetherness required of the task. As a result, they may view their fellow employees as "not carrying their share of the load," "waiting for someone else to get them going," or "too dependent on their fellow workers." The group work environment that relies strongly on a teamwork approach leads to a great deal of dissatisfaction for persons who prefer to work alone.

"The individuals to whom organization is a high preference will prefer a work setting in which the tasks to be accomplished are clearly outlined and there is a logical sequence of activities. These individuals may become frustrated in a work situation where the general sequence of events is often interrupted and results in realignment of the originally planned sequence. Attention to detail is a preference for some individuals and they prefer jobs in which detail is important. In those jobs where generalizations are more important than detail they will become "bogged down" in trying to extricate the details from the tasks. Thus they spend more time than needed to complete the task, and they expend time and energy trying to explain to fellow workers or supervisors the details they have uncovered that they believe to be highly important. To the fellow employees or supervisors these persons are often evaluated as less productive, a slower workers, etc. At the same time, these individuals cannot understand the other workers' attitudes of disregard for the details they believe are so important. These people would find greater job satisfaction in a work setting that utilized their preference for attention to detail.

"A preference for getting to know the instructor, having a mutual understanding and liking one another is very important for some students. For those students to whom this is very important, and due to a lack of understanding of this characteristic, these students often call those to whom it is important, "apple polishers." Likewise in the job setting many employees want to know their supervisor, have a mutual understanding and like one another. Attaining a good relationship with their supervisor contributes to their job satisfaction. Similarly in the job setting as in the student-teacher setting, strong criticism of "apple polishing" results from fellow employees to whom this characteristic is not important toward the one to whom it is. This kind of criticism, carried over a period of time, creates dissatisfaction among the group of workers. An understanding of this characteristic by the group of employees working under a supervisor can alleviate much of the criticism. This characteristic may vary from one company to another. Individuals applying for jobs can therefore attain this information through asking questions related to this characteristic during the job interview.

"The individuals who have a high preference for authority often desire classroom discipline and order or having informed, knowledgeable instructors. In the job setting, employees prefer an employer or supervisor who monitors the company policies, rules and regulations and in a sense "keeps everybody in line." Or if they define authority as "informed and knowledgeable" they expect their employers or supervisors to be able to answer their job related questions or be able to step in and perform their assigned task as well as they can.

"If goal setting is an important characteristic for individuals their job satisfaction will be enhanced if they are given the freedom and responsibility to set some of their own goals. Some individuals may want to be able to entirely set their own goals and thereby would prefer to be in a work setting that would allow this. Others may be satisfied or even prefer to be able to set personal achievement goals within the context of a larger overall goal of a company or organization. Yet others would prefer the goals be set and just be told what they are.

"Competition defined as desiring comparison with others, knowing how one is doing in relation to others, is another characteristic and one we are often told is very important in our overall society as well as the business world. However, while some students thrive on competition, we find many students who will retreat when competition in the classroom gets too high. In the world of work there are jobs that are highly competitive and others where competition is not so great. It is probably impossible to say that there are any jobs where there is never any competition but it may fit into job patterns in different ways. Some may meet the competition by developing a skill to a level of competence that they will be assured of attaining a good job. They are confident that they have acquired that skill to a greater degree than many others. Once on the job, they continue to build greater competence in that skill which they explain in terms of performing their job better. This can be defined as a kind of competition. People tend to refer to this kind of competition as internal competition or competition with oneself. External competition is comparing oneself to another person and trying to be better at a skill in order to produce more than the other person. Some kinds of jobs require some measure of competition all the way up the scale to those that are highly competitive. To the individuals for whom competition is a preference, job success may be measured in how well they compare to their fellow employees and if, in their judgment, they compare favorable it brings them satisfaction in their job. On the other hand, this kind of competition brings dissatisfaction to individuals with a low preference in this area. These people tend to refer to highly competitive activities as a real "rat race" and develop great dissatisfaction in those kinds of jobs.

"The groups of characteristics Canfield lists under content are preference for numeric, qualitative, inanimate, and people. Preferences for these kinds of activities are often identified through interest tests or aptitude tests. Most students can readily identify which of these characteristics they prefer without any kind of assessment administered to them.

"Through past experiences with subjects they have taken, students can relate whether or not they have a high preference for numeric which is working with numbers and logic, computing, solving mathematic problems, etc. Qualitative is a preference for working with words or language as in writing, editing or talking. Inanimate refers to working with things, buildings, repairing, designing, or operating. Those who prefer working with people prefer jobs where there is a great deal of people interaction such as interviewing, counseling, selling, and helping.

"Mode is the group of characteristics that identifies the way an individual prefers to receive information. The four on Canfield's Learning Styles Inventory are listening, reading, iconic, and direct experience. Listening is receiving information through lectures, speakers, etc. Reading is gaining information through the printed word. Iconic is interpreting charts and graphs or viewing illustrations, movie slides, and pictures. Direct experience is receiving information or gaining knowledge through handling or performing in the shop, the laboratory or on field trips, etc. At first glance these may seem to be only classroom activities. But when we do a thorough job analysis and take into consideration the kinds of activities performed on that job and the way individuals on that job receive their information or directions and keep updated, we begin to see the importance of this group of characteristics. Some jobs or companies may schedule regular briefing sessions, instructional periods or training sessions and deliver the information through lectures. Some may rely on much information to be relayed by telephone, etc.—all relying on listening. Other occupations may distribute their information through the printed word, thereby relying on reading not only for immediate pertinent information but for keeping the individual updated on new techniques, supplies, etc.

"Certain occupations may present a great deal of their information through charts and graphs or expect individuals to gain much information through reading blueprints or similar kinds of drawings which would be iconic. Other occupations may rely more on direct experience—gaining information through handling, performing or doing things in a shop or laboratory which might be commonly found in a manufacturing type setting. The direct experience through what we would call the field trip in the classroom setting could be an important characteristic for occupations which rely on observation such as our police force and investigative types of occupations.

"The characteristic Canfield identifies as expectancy identifies how well students expect to achieve. While this really is intended for achievement in the classroom setting there may be some carry-over into how successful individuals expect to be in the world of work. The self-fulfilling prophecy often hinders the ones who have the capability but do not expect to be successful. On the other hand, a high expectation of success without the necessary skills can be misleading. Therefore, it would be wise to counsel with your clients so that all things considered, their expectations for success will be parallel with the skills and abilities they have. The expectancy scale may need special attention when working with disadvantaged and handicapped individuals. For the most part, they do not achieve as well in school. They also have a history of failure so their expectation scale is often very low.

"In using the Learning Styles Inventory as a counseling tool, one needs to identify the strongest preferences from the condition, content and mode groups and compare these characteristics to those characteristics identified in a thorough job analysis or task analysis of specific occupations. To evaluate the probability of work satisfaction for individuals the work setting may need to be more clearly defined since occupations are often described in rather general terms. To explain this further, individuals may prefer working with numbers, attention to detail, prefer working with peers, and dislike working alone. They may have decided they really like bookkeeping and maybe would like to be a CPA. While this is quite simplified it may serve to express a point. They say they like bookkeeping. Their learning style shows they prefer working with numbers and they like detail. That is all very well and important for a CPA. One problem—they really dislike working alone and much prefer working with peers. They may want to look at occupations where they can use these skills but in those areas of the occupation where there may be more peer interaction—maybe something in the area of auditing or being a bank examiner."

Personal Role

Life-Style—Adler.   To help you to identify and understand the images you form of your clients from a personal role perspective, we suggest the work of Adler (Dinkmeyer, Pew, and Dinkmeyer, 1979). According to Adlerian psychology, individuals can be understood only in terms of their social environment. All behavior is purposive; that is, individuals try to find their place in the social environment. They have their own unique private logic for dealing with the milieu.

According to Adler an individual must respond to three major life tasks: (1) work, (2) society, and (3) sex. Solving problems in these life-task areas is a life-long process. Each person must find solutions to these problems in living. Adler believes that problems in these three areas cannot be solved separately, for they are intertwined. A change in one influences the others as well. A difficulty with one part of life implies comparable difficulties in the rest of one's life.

Individuals are not always aware of their approach toward life or how they are endeavoring to find their place. They usually are not able to understand the underlying consistencies that exist, and they often choose to dwell on apparent contradictions to explain away their failure to have complete self-understanding. This imperfection is understandable because one cannot be a participant and observer at the same time. In order to be helpful to someone it is often necessary to clarify the person's fundamental approach toward problems of life.

A basic contention of Adlerian psychology is that personality and character traits are expressions of movement within the family group. The concept of the family constellation as a dynamic explanation sees the development not so much the result of factors that converge on the individual, but that of one's own interpretation and related interaction. Each individual family member influences the group and the other members of the family as much as the member is influenced by them. Each member of the family has early relationships with other members and establishes ways to approach others in an effort to gain a place in the group. All strivings are directed toward a feeling of belonging.

An individual's experiences in the family, the opportunities and barriers, challenges and expectations, ambitions and frustrations are strongly influenced by one's position in the birth order of the family. Of greatest concern in this relationship is the impact of the family on the behavior patterns of the child. These experiences in the family are the most important determinants for one's frame of reference for perceiving, interpreting, and evaluating the world outside of the family. The knowledge, habits, and skills that the individual acquires in the home largely determine his or her capacity for dealing with outside situations as Pepper explains*:

Different individuals react differently to the same situation. No two children born into the same family grow up in the same situation. The family environment that surrounds each child is altered. In the life-pattern of every individual there is the imprint of one's position in the family with its definite characteristics. It is just upon this one fact, the individual's place

---

* Adapted from F. C. Pepper, "Birth Order," in *Techniques for Behavior Change,* ed. A. G. Nickelly (Springfield, Ill.: Charles C Thomas, 1971), pp. 50–53. Use with permission.

in the family constellation, that much of his or her future attitude toward life depends. No style of life is a unity because it has grown out of the difficulties of early life and out of the striving for a goal.

From the moment of birth individuals act, think, and feel in response to their world in accordance with how they experience or perceive their world (reality). What actually happens is not as important as how the situation is interpreted. The person's position in the family sequence is not the decisive factor, but rather the situation as the individual interprets it. The following hypotheses are based on ordinal position placement.

Single Child. The only child has a decidedly difficult start in life because the entire childhood is spent among persons who are more proficient. The only child may try to develop skills in areas that will gain approval of the adult world or solicit their sympathy.

- Is either a pampered child or a competent child.
- Enjoys a position as the center of interest.
- Sometimes has a feeling of insecurity due to the anxiety of the parents.
- Usually is not taught to gain things by own effort; merely to want something is to have it.
- Loners often expect a special place without having earned it.
- Often good independent readers because reading is a way of being the center of attention unless solicitous parents create anxiety.

Oldest Child. The oldest child has a threatened position in life; being the oldest should entitle the first child to have the favored spot and frequently does. However, he or she may become discouraged upon the birth of the second child and refuse to accept responsibility.

- Is an only child for a period of time and has, therefore, been the center of interest.
- Has to be first in the sense of gaining and holding superiority over the next children. Superior school performance may be a way of demonstrating ability.
- Becomes a "dethroned" child with a birth of the second child. May feel unloved and neglected. Usually strives to keep or to regain attention by positive deeds.
- Can develop a good, competent behavior pattern or become extremely discouraged (may develop good reading skills or need remedial work).

If the oldest child is a boy followed by a sister within a short time:

- Girls develop faster than boys during ages one to seventeen and press closely on the heels of the first child. Girls may displace boy as "oldest" child.
- The boy usually tries to assert himself because of cultural expectations for boys and may take advantage of his masculine role.
- As a teenager, may become a critic of parents whereas previously he was critical only of siblings.

Second Child. The second child has somewhat of an uncomfortable position in life and usually takes a steam-engine attitude, trying to catch up with the child in front and has feelings of being under constant pressure.

- Never has the parents' undivided attention.
- Always has another child in front who is more advanced.
- Feels that the first child cannot be beaten, which disputes a claim of equality.
- Often acts as though there is a race to be won. Hyperactive and pushy, described as having a short attention span when in reading tasks.
- Has the "Avis-complex"—because I am second I will try harder.
- If the first child is successful, the second is more likely to feel uncertain of self.
- Usually is the opposite of the first child.
- Becomes a "squeezed child" whenever a third child is born.
- Tends to be more aggressive socially than oldest child.
- Lacks word attack skills, will guess at words and move on to something else.

Youngest Child. The youngest child has a peculiar place in the family constellation and may become a "speeder" because of being outdistanced and thus may become the most successful; or if discouraged may have inferiority feelings.

- Is often like an only child.
- Usually things are done for the "baby"—decisions made and responsibility taken.
- Usually is spoiled by the family.
- Finds oneself in an embarrassing position—(is usually the smallest, the weakest and, above all,—not taken seriously).
- May become the "boss" in the family.
- Either attempts to excel the brothers and sisters or evades the direct struggle for superiority.
- May retain the baby role and hook others into a service role.
- Often allies with the first as being different from the rest.
- Prefers others to help with reading, may like to read aloud to become a center of attention.

Middle Child of Three. The middle child of three has an uncertain place in the family group and may feel neglected. The middle child discovers that neither the privileges of the youngest nor the rights of the older child is available.

- May feel unloved and abused.
- Becomes a "squeezed child" when third child is born.
- May hold the conviction that people are unfair.
- May be unable to find a place in the group.
- May become extremely discouraged and prone to become a problem child.
- Views learning tasks as an imposition, something to avoid because others are successful.

Bradley (1982) made some interesting observations in relating birth order to career decisions. He points out that out of the first twenty-three U.S. astronauts who traveled into space, twenty-one were either only children or firstborns; a sample of attorneys found 66% were firstborns; about the same overrepresentation for members of Congress; another study found a significantly higher incidence of firstborns among physicians, teachers, and nurses. It seems that firstborns are responsive to parental expectations and cultural values.

Secondborns tend to be less duty bound and therefore will be more casual and unconventional. Studies related to creativity found fewer firstborns as creative writers; secondborns scored 2.5 times higher in creativity tasks than firstborns in two-child families. (There was variability in larger-sized families.) Age spacing between siblings is an important factor. With five to six years' separation between children ordinal position starts to take on new meaning; with ten to twelve years, the separation effects are usually well determined. A large age separation means that each child is raised like a firstborn or only child.

Toman (1969) stresses age spacing in predicting adult personal-social relationships. Toman also adds the compounding factor of sexual role expectations. Children of the same sex who are one to four years apart are likely to be the most competitive. Sex role expectations provide additional means for children to find their place in the family system. Children spaced six years or more apart and of the opposite sex are likely to be the least competitive. Directional strivings are accentuated by sex roles. For example, if the good student or scholar is a girl and the next child is a boy, a masculine role may be sought, such as being an athlete or an automotive buff.

Another way to view life-styles (a person's style of acting, thinking, and perceiving), and hence the themes by which an individual lives, is to look at types of behavior. As you are involved in career counseling with clients here are some possible behaviors you may observe. The language used maybe helpful as you gather together the images of your clients and group them into life career themes.

LIFE-STYLE THEMES*

1. The *getter* actively or passively manipulates life and others by employing charm, shyness, temper, or intimidation to put others into his or her service.

2. The *driver* is the person perpetually in motion, the overconscientious, over-ambitious person constantly striving to complete a goal. Each day is viewed in terms of how best to get the most mileage with as few pit stops as possible. Life is a perpetual race for such persons, although the goal or finish line is

* Adapted from H. H. Mosak, "Lifestyle," in *Techniques for Behavior Change* (Springfield, Ill.: Charles C Thomas, 1971), pp. 78–80. Used with permission.

seldom attained. As one individual stated, "I don't know where I'm going, but I've got my foot to the floorboard."

3. The *controller* either wants to control life or is afraid that it will dominate him or her. Surprises are disliked, spontaneity controlled, and feelings largely masked or hidden from others. Intellectualism, rightness, orderliness, and neatness are favored actions. Such a person is always concerned about "saying the right thing at the right time."

4. Persons who need to be *right* scrupulously avoid making errors. Should they be caught in an error, they often will rationalize that others are wrong more often than they are. Being right becomes an obsession.

5. People who need to be *superior* may refuse to enter life tasks in which they cannot be the center or the best. Such people may engage in such socially nonconstructive activities as seeing how many consecutive times they can jump on a pogo stick for the purpose of breaking the world record. If they cannot be first or best, they may settle for last or worst.

6. People who need to be *liked* and please everybody all the time are sensitive to criticism and feel crushed when not enjoying universal and constant approval. They are adept at discovering how to be accepted by others, and feel that such opinions are the only measure of their personal worth.

7. People who need to be *good* prefer living by higher moral standards than their peers. Such extreme goodness may serve as an instrument for moral superiority, so that such persons not only elevate themselves over others, but may actually discourage the inferior person. As Mosak notes, this is a frequent device of the model child or the alcoholic's spouse.

8. People who *oppose everything* rarely can be found to be *for* anything. They are quick to identify faults, constantly finding themselves opposed to the programs or desires of others.

9. The *victim* innocently or actively becomes a disaster chaser, characterized by feelings of nobility, self-pity, resignation, or proneness to accident. Seeking the sympathy or pity of others is also commonly employed by such people.

10. The *martyr* is similar to the victim, except that his or her death is for a noble or righteous cause. Moral indignation and silent suffering at the hands of unjust others are common actions.

11. The *baby* finds a place through the use of charm, cuteness, and exploitation of others. Often (but not always) the youngest in the family constellation, such persons may have high-pitched voices and childlike mannerisms employed to put others into their service.

12. The *inadequate* person can do nothing right, being thoroughly awkward or clumsy. Often activities are limited to those in which some success is guaranteed, and assuming responsibility generally results in failure. Such a person loudly proclaims his or her own inadequacies, a living symbol of an inferiority complex.

13. People who *avoid feelings* believe that logical thinking and rational living can solve all life's problems. Their most prized characteristics consist of their logic, rationalization, intellectualization, and talking a good game.

14. The *excitement seeker* despises dull, routine activities, preferring constant thrill and motion. In searching for excitement, others are often employed in providing new exhilaration. "Let's party tonight" is a frequent theme. Some excitement seekers, however, do not involve others and find excitement through fears and rumination.

Hemispheric Functioning

Still another way to bring together in theme form the images you have of your clients as a result of career counseling is to use a hemispheric functioning model. The human brain has two sides to it, two hemispheres, that are connected at the center. Split-brain research has shown that the left and right hemispheres process information in different ways. How and why the hemispheres function more or less independently or in an integrated fashion is still unknown. Some speculation suggests functioning may be partially determined by blood supply to the two hemispheres. Other speculation postulates that the educational process might be a primary factor. The hemispheres also may be specialized for the kind of thought or information processing the person chooses to use. There is always the possibility that there are some evolutionary basis as the split. Nevertheless, the need to simplify has caused some persons to be overzealous in applying hemispheric functioning findings. While we should guard against over generalization (Robbins, 1985) "the idea of the brain having two different hemispheres is valuable to use as a metaphor, even if that metaphor is highly simplistic . . . as a statement of actual reality" (Bolles, 1982, p. 2).

What Is Known.   The human nervous system is connected to the brain in a crossed-over fashion. The left hemisphere controls the right side of the body; the right hemisphere controls the left side. Because of this crossing over of the nerve pathways, the left hand is connected to the right hemisphere; the right hand, to the left hemisphere. This means that if the left side of the brain is damaged, the right side of the body might be paralyzed or impaired.

What about other human functions that depend on the brain? It seems that each hemisphere specializes even though the function could be carried out by either half. The basic two dimensions appear to be time and space. As we process information in terms of time (left mode), we are perceiving things sequentially, forming a basis for logical thinking. When we use space (right mode) to process information, we perceive things holistically, forming a basis for intuition and creative thinking.

The left hemisphere appears to be "prewired" genetically to organize language, to use symbols, to store language information, to learn values, and to provide the seat of socialization capabilities. However, the right side of the brain is better at spatial problems—arranging shapes to match a design, for example. The right hemisphere seems to involve a range of nonverbal integrative functions including holistic perception, space and form perception, directional orientation, and visual imagery.

We know that despite our normal feeling that we are one person—a single being—our brains are double, each half with its own way of knowing, its own way of perceiving external reality. It is fortunate that the two hemispheres can work together in a number of ways. Each hemisphere can contribute its special abilities toward a task; the hemispheres can work singularly, with one half "on" and the other half "off."

The hemispheres may conflict when one half attempts to do what the other half "knows" it can do better. Also, each half seems to be able to keep knowledge from the other. What does this mean? We have a double brain with two ways of knowing. As each of our hemispheres gathers the same sensory information, each half may handle the part of the information suited to its style or specialization, or one hemisphere may take over and inhibit the other half. This dominance is usually by the left hemisphere because it tends to specialize in keeping things in order. The left hemisphere analyzes, counts, marks time, plans step-by-step procedures, verbalizes, and makes rational statements based on logic; it figures things out.

The second way of knowing (the right hemisphere) exists in the mind's eye. We "see" things with imagery or recall things that may be real (can you imagine your bedroom?). We see how things exist in space and how the parts go together to make up the whole. Using the right hemisphere, we dream; we use music and other sounds to form images; we use touch and our sense of smell to create "moods"; we create new combinations of ideas. Gestures are often related to right-hemisphere communication—(try to describe a spiral staircase without making a spiral gesture.) The right hemisphere uses intuition and insight; everything comes together or falls into place.

One of the capabilities of the right hemisphere is imagining—seeing an imaginary picture with your mind's eye. The brain is able to conjure an image and then "look" at it, "seeing" it as if it is really there. Imagining connotes a still picture, but we can also visualize moving images. Visualizing is like watching movies in our mind's eye.

The two hemispheres most likely use and put together information into meaningful wholes so that individuals can totally perceive and understand their environment. In essence, the major function of this specialization is the final integration of information from both hemispheres into one meaningful whole. For example, in reading and writing individuals must integrate information from both hemispheres, not only to recognize and understand the activity, but also to continue to produce verbal and motoric expression. This specialization and eventual integration is perhaps the key to higher human capabilities.

HEMISPHERE LATERALIZATION

Left Hemisphere	Right Hemisphere
Time	Space
Sequential	Holistic
Logical	Intuitive

Analyzes	Creates
Intellectualizes	Imagines
Symbolic	Sensory
Verbal	Kineasthetic
Planful	Impulsive
Rules	Risks
Controlled	Emotional
Technical	Artistic
Organizing	Sythesizing
Socialized	Impetuous
Realistic	Inventive
Ordered	Rhythmic
Digital	Analogic

Implications for Life Career Theme Analysis.   The assessment of hemispheric functioning has not received much attention until recently. Some practitioners have attempted to adapt tests such as the WAIS and WISC-R to identify hemispheric preferences and skills. However, many of the verbal scales normally associated with left-brain functioning also require right-brain functions, such as visualization and spatial orientation, while many of the performance scales normally associated with right-brain functioning also require left-brain functions, such as logical analysis and temporal sequencing.

Reynolds et al. (1979) used self-report procedures to provide perceived preferences of individuals. They asked respondents to choose from such choices as:

a. I am good at remembering faces.
b. I am good at remembering names.
c. I am just as good at remembering names as I am remembering faces.
a. I like to learn facts like names and dates.
b. I like to learn about what people think might happen someday.
c. I like to learn facts like names and dates just as well as learning about what people think might happen someday.

Similarly, Hill's (1976) Educational Cognitive Style Interest Inventory contains items requiring a choice from the usually, sometimes, and rarely categories.

A story is easier to understand in a movie than in a book.
I prefer to have directions written on the board as they are being explained.
I work best in an organized situation.

Fadely and Hosler (1979) provide an observation guide aimed as evaluating school-aged children. Examples follow that are rated on a five-point scale.

Category:	Time orientation
Sample item:	Uses time to organize self.
Category:	Abstract thought
Sample item:	Can apply rules to abstract thought.
Category:	Holistic and gestalt
Sample item:	Remembers visual aspects of people objects but forgets names

As you work with clients we suggest that you consider the Fadely and Hosler (1979) framework for understanding hemispheric functioning. It seems to be the most useful when grouping client images into themes. The following are the categories around which you can group themes.

LEFT MODE CHARACTERISTICS	RIGHT MODE CHARACTERISTICS
Verbally expressive	Motorically expressive
Logical	Intuitive
Orderly and sequential	Holistic and gestalt
Time orientation	Spatial orientation
Socialized values	Naturalistic values
Aggressive-assertive	Submissive-accepting
Abstract thought	Concrete thought
Vertical thought—structured	Lateral thought—creative
Objective	Subjective
Conventional motor organization	Mixed and unconventional motor organization

Implications for Career Counseling. In addition to the above implications concerning how ideas about hemispheric functioning can be useful in theme identification and grouping, these ideas also have implications for career counseling:

1. If you use a skills identification teachnique with a client, make sure that skills in both hemispheres are accounted for. The reason for this is that we tend to focus on skills in our favored hemisphere and ignore skills in our less favored hemisphere. For example, highly verbal people may identify left hemisphere skills such as analyzing, organizing, dissecting, and thinking logically, but ignore right hemisphere skills such as intuition, body awareness, and artistic abilities. Likewise, artistic people may notice skills in the right hemisphere such as recognition of pitch, the ability to compose, dream interpretation, and the ability to picture things, but ignore left hemisphere skills such as the ability to analyze, think logically, and do mathematical computations (Bolles, 1982, pp. 4–5).

2. The planning of educational and training programs could be aided by attention to the client's *preferred learning mode.* Individuals with left mode preferences like lectures, discussions, and perhaps programmed materials. Those with right mode preferences like iconic displays, demonstrations, and hands-on experiences.

3. Many career counseling approaches are dominated by left hemispheric strategies that use words, analyze parts, and evolve sequential step-by-step action plans. Traditional uses of occupational and labor market information are usually organized around left mode strategies. In addition to these strategies, you may wish to help clients become involved in career exploration through right-mode strategies including imagery, metaphors/stories, and direct situations/face-to-face experiences (Bolles, 1982, p. 4).

4. Although many people have little difficulty using both hemispheres, some individuals need help in learning how to use both hemispheres. This involves influencing left-hemisphere-dominant individuals to integrate right mode usage and right-hemisphere-dominant individuals to incorporate left mode usage. Since this process is developmental it can be accomplished only with clients with whom you have contact over a period of time. Moving from the left mode dominance to right mode usage is easier because the "freeing" process is usually more enjoyable than a right-to-left change because that change involves the hard work of disciplining oneself. Creating images and the like can be stimulating, but the task of analysis, control, and ordering is similar to in school.

PRACTICE IN IDENTIFYING THEMES

Since the concept of themes is abstract, it is more difficult to explain than it is to demonstrate by example. Although some examples were provided throughout the chapter, more are given below. As explained previously, themes are ideas, beliefs, attitudes, and values that people hold about themselves, others, and the world at large. These *I am, others are,* and *life is* statements have a lot to do with peoples' behavior. By looking at behavior— both words and actions—life career themes can be inferred or directly observed (Mosak, 1971).

Examples of Themes

What follows are some examples of statements clients might make during career counseling activities and the possible themes these statements might represent.

CLIENT STATEMENTS	POSSIBLE THEMES
To have a job that provides many extra fringe benefits	To receive direct benefits
To receive a large yearly pay increase or bonus	
To have a job which provides personal comfort and good working conditions	
To have ample work breaks or get time off	
To be able to manage money or resources	

To be my own boss	To be independent
To be free to make my own decisions	
To be directly responsible to no one at work	
To work with little supervision	
To be free to vary my working hours	
To be able to question the customary way of doing things	To achieve ideals
To be able to explore various aspects of a job	
To discuss which of a number of alternatives better explains a situation	
To believe the work I do is important or significant to others	
To be able to consider myself a creative person	
To know exactly how my supervisors expect a job to be done	To be responsible
To be able to see the results of my work at the end of each day	
To be able to measure how much work I have done	
To know the problem on which I am working has a correct solution	
To know that when I have finished a task, it is done once and for all	
To size up a person or situation for decision making	To provide leadership
To be responsible for making major decisions that affect the work of other people	
To be responsible for hiring and firing people	
To coordinate the work of others	
To be able to verbally influence a group of people	
To know a large number of the people with whom I work	To have social contact
To be around workers of the same age and interests	
To be spoken well of by supervisors	
To know and associate with fellow workers	
To have other workers ask for my personal advice	

To make a deal with someone	To negotiate
To find ways to settle an argument	
To act on gut reactions	
To confer with people about solving problems	
To listen and bring understanding to both sides of an argument	
To keep records, inventory, or charts and make appointments	To organize
To collect information, gather materials or samples	
To calculate, compute, or manipulate numbers	
To classify information or organize it into categories	
To move something into place; to remove or repair	To handle
To examine, inspect, and handle with precision	
To groom, make up, or work with precision	
To work, smooth out, grind, stress, press materials and products	
To do my best work the room must be free of distractions	To establish routine
To have an established daily routine	
To have chores done on a regular schedule	
To arrange my time so that each task is done at the same time every day	
To allow me to work on one task at a time	
To be physically active	To be active
To participate in outdoor sports	
To have hobbies and interests involving muscular coordination	
To be involved in doing something active	

REFERENCES

BANDLER, R., and GRINDLER, J., *The Structure of Magic*. Palo Alto, Calif.: Science and Behavior Books, 1975.

BLOCHER, D. H., "Some Implications of Recent Research in Social and Developmental Psychology for Counseling Practice," *The Personnel and Guidance Journal*, 58, no. 5 (1980).

BOLLES, R. N., *The Three Boxes of Life*. Berkeley, Calif.: Ten Speed Press, 1981.

———, "The Significance of the Brain for Career Counseling and Job Hunting," *Newsletter about Life/Work Planning*, no. 3, (1982).

———, *What Color is Your Parachute?* Berkeley, Calif.: Ten Speed Press, 1985.

———, and ZENOFF, V. B., *The Quick Job-Hunting Map*. Berkeley, Calif.: Ten Speed Press, 1977.

BRADLEY, R. W., "Using Birth Order and Sibling Dynamics in Career Counseling," *The Personnel and Guidance Journal*, 61, no. 1 (1982).

CAFFERTY, E., "Learning Style as a Tool in Career Guidance." Paper presented at the American Vocational Association Convention, December 6, 1980.

CANFIELD, A. A., *Learning Style Inventory*. Plymouth, Mich.: Humanics, Inc., 1977.

DINKMEYER, D. C., PEW, W. L. and DINKMEYER, D. C. *Adlerian Counseling and Psychotherapy*. Montery, Calif.: Brooks/Cole, 1979.

DREIKURS, R., "The Holistic Approach: Two Points of a Line," in *Education, Guidance, Psychodynamics*, Proceedings of the Conference of the Individual Psychology Association of Chicago. Chicago: Alfred Adler Institute, 1966.

FADELY, J. L., and HOSLER, V. N., *Understanding the Alpha Child at Home and School*. Springfield, Ill.: Charles C Thomas, 1979.

GERBER, A., JR. "Finding the Car in Career," *Journal of Career Education*, 9 (1983), 181–183.

HILL, J. E., *Cognitive Style as an Educational Science*. Oakland, Mich.: Oakland Community College, 1976.

HOLLAND, J. L., *Making Vocational Choices: A Theory of Vocational Personalities and Work Environments* (2nd ed.). Englewood Cliffs, N.J.: Prentice-Hall, 1985.

IVEY, A. E., and SIMEK-DOWNING, L., *Counseling and Psychotherapy: Skills, Theories, and Practice*. Englewood Cliffs, N.J.: Prentice-Hall, 1980.

KELLEY, G. A., *The Psychology of Personal Constructs, Vol. 1, A Theory of Personality*. New York: W. W. Norton, 1955.

KOLB, D. A., *The Learning Style Inventory: Technical Manual*. Boston: McBer and Company, 1976.

———, *Experiential Learning*. Englewood Cliffs, N.J.: Prentice-Hall, 1984.

MOSAK, H. H., "Lifestyle," in *Techniques For Behavior Change*, ed. A. G. Nikelly. Springfield, Ill.: Charles C Thomas, 1971.

NICKELLY, A. G., ed. *Techniques for Behavior Change*, Springfield, Ill.: Charles C Thomas, 1971.

PREDIGER, D. J., "A World of Work Map for Career Exploration," *The Vocational Guidance Quarterly*, 24, no. 3 (1976).

———, "Mapping Occupations and Interests: A Graphic Aid for Vocational Guidance and Research," *The Vocational Guidance Quarterly*, 30, no. 1 (1981).

REYNOLDS, C. R., KALTSONNIS, B., and TORRANCE, E. P., "A Children's Form of Your Style of Learning and Thinking: Preliminary Norms and Technical Data," *The Gifted Child Quarterly*, 22, no. 4 (1979).

ROBBINS, S. B., "Left-Right Brain Research and Its Premature Generalization to the Counseling Setting," *Journal of Counseling and Development*, 64, no. 4 (1985).

SUNDBERG, N. D., *Assessment of Persons*. Englewood Cliffs, N.J.: Prentice-Hall, 1977.

TOMAN, W., *Family Constellation* (2nd ed.). New York: Springer Publishing Co., 1969.

U.S. Department of Labor, *Dictionary of Occupational Titles* (4th ed.). Washington, D.C.: U.S. Government Printing Office, 1977.

WOLFE, D. M., and KOLB, D. A., "Career Development, Personal Growth, and Experiential Learning," in *Issues in Career and Human Resource Development*, ed. J. W. Springer. Madison, Wisc.: American Society for Training and Development, 1980.

A Structured Interview for Career Counseling

Rather than relying on abstract psychological characteristics to explain and predict human work preferences and behaviors, it is possible to maximize and capitalize on an individual's real, everyday work experiences as these accumulate over the life span. This involves helping people to evaluate the impact of concrete events as they occur in real life. (Berman and Munson, 1981, p. 96)

In the first two chapters you were introduced to a framework for career counseling and some skills that can help you understand and interpret certain types of client information and behavior. You also have been introduced to the concept of identifying and analyzing life career themes and some skills involved in carrying out these processes. The next step is to introduce you to a structured interview that can be used during the first phase of career counseling to surface and provide a structure for client self- and environmental information.

Chapter 3 first presents a description of this structured interview called the life career assessment (LCA). Then the theory and structure of the LCA are presented. Following this, specific attention is given to how the family role and family issues can be explored using the LCA. The chapter closes with some ideas about using the LCA with a variety of clients.

WHAT IS THE LIFE CAREER ASSESSMENT?

The life career assessment (LCA) is a structured interview technique that you may wish to consider using when you first meet with your clients. The LCA does not take much time. In fact, the entire interview can be completed in thirty to forty-five minutes. If necessary, it can be divided into ten- to fifteen-minute sections and used over several contacts with clients.

The LCA is designed to cover clients' levels of functioning in various life roles including the worker, learner, and personal roles as well as yielding information on how they negotiate their environments. The LCA helps you form positive relationships with clients. An atmosphere of concern and caring can be created by the nonjudgmental, nonthreatening, conversational tone of the LCA. Printed forms, booklets, and paper-and-pencil instruments, which some clients may associate negatively with school, training, and evaluation, are not used.

The LCA helps to increase clients' career planning abilities. The discovery, through the LCA, of their strengths and the obstacles they may face and their levels of functioning in various arenas of life may suggest goals to establish, which in turn can lead to action to reach these goals. These discoveries also may suggest the use of career assessment tools, such as standardized tests, by revealing problem areas that need further exploration and by uncovering skills and abilities that may require further evaluation.

THEORY OF THE LCA

The LCA will help you and your clients understand the relation your clients have to their environment. It is based on the individual psychology of Adler (Dinkmeyer, Pew, and Dinkmeyer, 1979). He divides an individual's relation to the world into three life tasks: (1) work, (2) society (social relations), and (3) sex (friendship). According to Adler the three tasks cannot be dealt with separately since they are intertwined. A change in one involves the others as well. Difficulty in one part of life implies comparable difficulties in the rest of life. Although it may appear otherwise, a person's life is usually quite integrated.

People tend to solve problems and attempt to obtain rewards or satisfaction in a similar manner in all three arenas. We use the phrase *life career themes* to describe these consistent ways of negotiating with the world. You will recall we defined themes as the ways people express ideas, beliefs, attitudes, and values about themselves, others, and the world in general. There are many different themes by which people operate, and each individual will tend to operate using a number of themes. The themes individuals use can be considered to constitute a life-style. Individuals are not always aware of their approach toward life or the themes by which they operate, and they may not recognize the underlying consistencies that exist (Mosak, 1971). They may choose, rather, to dwell on specific, superficial feelings that serve to further obscure the way in which they are developing.

In the following dialogue a client is talking about her past job experiences. The participant in this interview is a twenty-five-year-old woman enrolled in an employment and training program. Notice the possible themes that can be identified from this brief discussion.

DIALOGUE	THEMES
CO: Let's find out about your work experience. Could you tell me about your last job?	
CL: It was with a small insurance company. I was in the claims department. I sent out form letters and payment checks.	
CO: What did you like about the job?	
CL: It was alright, but it was kind of boring. There wasn't much excitement to it. All the people were quite a bit older than I was. I was the youngest one. They were all real nice. It was alright.	Looking to work around others the same age so she can socialize.
CO: What are some things you really liked about that job?	
CL: The people were real nice even though they were older. I liked talking on the phone to all the different people. That's mainly why I got into claims, so that I could talk to people and wouldn't be all by myself. I liked working downtown where there's a lot of places to go and I liked the insurance business.	Likes social contact.
CO: Did you?	
CL: Yeah, I don't think I'd like car insurance, but I liked life and health insurance. It was pretty interesting. There were many different plans, and they were interesting to read.	
CO: What are some of the things you didn't like about it other than the older people working there?	
CL: I just had a set thing that I did every day. I'd check the mail, and I hated doing that and the form letters. I got to where that's all I could type were	Dislike for routine.

form letters. If I tried to type a letter that was handwritten, I just couldn't do it because I just wasn't used to it. And it was just dull, but other than that I liked it.

CO: What about the job you had before that?

CL: It was a floral company. I liked it real well. Mom had gone to school with the owners. I really liked those people. They were a lot of fun. I loved to work with flowers. When I was on delivery I got to go out and run around and I liked that. That was a pretty fun job

Contact with people is important.

CO: What about when you worked at the garment factory?

CL: Oh, I hated that. That was terrible. I worked at night. I went to school all day long and I worked until 1:00 in the morning. I just don't like to do all that routine stuff, that'll make a person go crazy. And I was on my feet all day long, and we got a 10 minute break and a half hour for lunch. It was just too much work.

Does not like to be closed in.

Recurring themes from this dialogue suggest that she enjoys working around people, especially to meet some of her social needs. She probably dislikes routine kinds of jobs, but can adapt to them if she is receiving other satisfaction. As important as learning what exact jobs she has held is learning what kind of working environment is most reinforcing for her. A major purpose of the LCA is to begin the process of helping clients clarify their fundamental approaches to life or the means by which they typically operate (themes).

Assessing your clients' approach to work, society (social relations), and sex (friendships) provides a concrete way of analyzing and synthesizing their movement in life. This assessment is a cooperative endeavor that not only helps you understand your clients, but also helps them better understand their own life themes that reveal their unique sense of the meaning of life. By identifying such themes through the LCA, you and your clients can begin to understand their approaches to life and do so in a comfortable and straightforward manner.

STRUCTURE OF THE LCA

The LCA structure is presented below in outline form. As you will see, there are four major sections: career assessment; typical day; strengths and obstacles; and summary. Each section is covered in detail in subsequent discussion in this chapter, but for now, a most important point to notice is that by following this format you can obtain several types of information. One type is relatively objective and factual regarding your clients' work experiences and educational achievements. Another type is your clients' estimations of the skills and competencies they possess. Still another type is inferences made by you of your clients' skills and abilities. These inferences are based on themes and are derived from the kinds of activities your clients are involved in at work, in school or training, or at leisure. Another kind of information obtained concerns your clients' opinions of their value as persons and their awareness of self. You also can begin to determine, through theme finding, your clients' approaches to life.

Although the LCA format is suggested for you to follow, there is no one prescribed way to use the format. You will need to discover your own personal style of using the LCA. In fact, it is preferable for you to integrate the LCA structure into your own style as well as the style of your clients to keep the process from becoming mechanical and to make the initial interviews as meaningful as they have the potential to be.

Career Assessment

1. Work experience (part/full-time, paid/unpaid)
   - Last job
   - Liked best about
   - Disliked most about
   - Same procedure with another job
2. Education or training progress and concerns
   - General appraisal
   - Liked best about
   - Disliked most about
   - Repeat for levels or types
3. Recreation
   - Leisure-time activities
   - Social life (within leisure context)
   - Friends (within leisure context)

Typical Day

1. Dependent-independent
   - Relies on others
   - Insists on someone else making decisions
2. Systematic-spontaneous
   - Stable routine
   - Persistent and attentive

Strengths and Obstacles

1. Three main strengths
   - Resources at own disposal
   - What do resources do for clients
2. Three main obstacles
   - Related to strengths
   - Related to themes

Summary

1. Agree on life themes
2. Use client's own words
3. Relate to goal setting

Career Assessment

The career assessment section of the interview is divided into three parts: (1) work experience, (2) education or training progress and concerns, and (3) recreation. Here is a bit more detail:

1. Work experience (part/full-time, paid/unpaid)
   - Last job
     Liked best about
     Disliked most about
   - Supervision
     Liked best about
     Disliked most about
   - Same procedure with another job
2. Education or training progress and concerns
   - General appraisal
     Liked best about school/learning
     Disliked most about school/learning
   - Subject preference
     Liked
     Disliked
   - Teacher or instructor characteristics (for example, closeness, authority)
     Liked
     Disliked
   - Classroom or training condition preferences
     Independent versus dependent study
     Contact with other students or trainees
     Learning mode
   - Repeat for levels
3. Recreation
   - Leisure-time activities
   - Social life (within leisure context)
   - Friends (within leisure context)
   - Weekends/weekdays, evenings

Work Experience.   To assess work experience ask your clients to describe their last or current job. The jobs can be part-time or full-time, paid or unpaid. Ask your clients to describe the tasks performed and then relate what was liked best and least about the jobs. As likes and dislikes are discussed, the themes that become apparent should be repeated, clarified, and reflected so that your clients are aware of the consistencies running through them. Examining your clients' domestic responsibilities, such as mowing the lawn, caring for a younger sibling, or doing household chores, also can be revealing and is especially useful when clients have had little or no work experience. This process is illustrated by the following example of an interview with a thirty-year-old client in which his work experience was discussed.

DIALOGUE	THEMES
CO: The county hospital was the last job you had? You were working in the kitchen. You worked there quite awhile?	
CL: Right at two years.	
CO: Did you work at night, all day, or evening?	
CL: Got up at 9:00 and went to work at 11:00 . . . the whole day was there. You don't see any sunshine and it's dark when you get out. I didn't like that too much. At first it was okay. But then I didn't want to work those hours. It seemed like the whole day. When I got really good at my job I got my work done by 3:00 or 2:00 and I would have to sit or help someone do odds and ends until 4:30 or 5:00. That really got tiring.	Does not like routine.
CO: What was your job exactly?	
CL: Work a tray line, patient tray line. Afterwards, clean up and then we have odds and ends to do like go up on the floors and take the floor ice cream, milk, bread, or fruit. Weigh fruit for the next meal. Just little odds and ends that you could get done once you knew what you were doing. They had a time schedule set, but me, once I	Takes care of details so that he can contact others.

got the hang of it, it didn't take
me the time schedule they had
for me, so I just went from one
thing to the next. And then I'd
get done at 3:00 or 2:30,
sometimes I'd get done at 2:00.
I'd help the other people.
Then, we all sit around till 4:30
till the next meal comes.

CO: You really like to keep busy   Completion of tasks is important.
   then. It seems like you like to
   have something to show for it.
CL: Otherwise I get bored with it.

The client's job priorities and life themes begin to emerge in this short excerpt, although there is still much to find out about his aspirations and current skills. Note that his need for variety may interfere with his performance in a routine job. This is something to discuss with him later when beginning to look at occupational options.

Education or Training Progress and Concerns.   To begin this section of the interview, ask your clients for a general appraisal of their educational or training experiences. You can provide further structure by asking what your clients liked best and liked least. Usually themes begin to appear as likes and dislikes. These themes should be repeated, clarified, and reflected so that your clients are aware of the consistencies or inconsistencies running through them.

After clients give you some general impressions about their educational background or their training experiences, you can begin to ask more specific questions about preferences for subjects, teachers, instructors, and learning conditions. This kind of focusing will yield several types of information. One kind is relatively factual and surface information, such as "I like science and math, and dislike art and English" or "I like Mr. Jones and Mrs. Green, but don't get along well with Mr. Smith." Another kind of focusing is on the themes discussed earlier, many of which will appear throughout the interview. You also can obtain clues regarding your clients' learning styles from this section of the LCA.

The following is an excerpt from an interview in which a client's school experience is discussed:

DIALOGUE   **THEMES**

CO: Tell me about your school
   experience.
CL: I liked it, until I got into eighth
   grade, I think it was, and then
   I just lost interest in it. Right
   around eighth grade.

CO: What happened then to make you lose interest?

CL: I have no idea. I guess I just kinda thought I knew everything and started running around.

CO: When you think back to elementary school, you said you liked it pretty well. What were some things that you remember liking, what was good?

CL: Um, in fourth grade I can always remember third and fourth grade . . . spelling and capitalization and stuff like that. We always had special games to make it a lot more fun, you know. The spelling bee. If you completed so many words right we got a star on the board. Things like that. I remember how the teacher always pointed me out as being the one person who always got the stars. I guess the things that I got rewards for made it more interesting.

Seeks rewards and recognition. Approval from adults is important.

CO: You felt like you could see that you had done something good. . . .

CL: She would have me help other people.

Seeks acceptance.

CO: You must have felt very worthwhile. Now tell me what you did *not* like about school.

CL: Well, my worst class was fifth grade.

CO: What was so bad about it?

CL: The teacher was an old mean thing. I'm not kidding! Can you imagine somebody reading, what was it . . . the story *Gone With the Wind*. I had to read that story in the fifth grade. That thing was about this thick and then she had me write a report.

Large assignments can be overwhelming.

CO: She made you do that as a punishment?

CL: We got off to a bad start, and when she did that to me it just made it worse. I went to the library or something and me and some girls were passing notes or something so as a punishment she gave us all these real big books to read . . . real hard books to read. Then I stuck a tack underneath her chair and somebody told on me. So for a month she would send home progress reports to my father and he would make me sit and write "I am sorry . . ." five hundred times each night. But sixth grade was a lot of fun. She liked to get outdoors and she always took us on field trips to the parks, make a whole afternoon of it. On the weekends she had this nice place out of town and she would always ask us if we wanted to come out on Saturday or Sunday. We would always go out there, if we needed help.

Attention from adults is important.
Acts out for revenge.
Needs involvement.

CO: Seemed like she really cared.

CL: Yeah, she was real nice. I think she left the next year.

CO: You said when you got to junior high you kind of lost interest.

CL: Seemed like once I got to junior high and high school nobody really took interest in what you were doing. That might have been part of it. I was used to the one class and everything. I'm kinda old fashioned.

Lacks assertiveness skills.
No adult attention brings loneliness.

CO: You felt you were left on your own with no one to go for help.

CL: That was a lot of it. Because I need a lot of help with the short time you've got there and all the students, I would leave class and still have questions. I

Lacks confidence and is dependent.

wouldn't know what to do the
next day. So I just got further
and further behind. I'll have
something to say, but I never
say it until it's too late. I
remember I talked to my
counselor.

CO: What did your counselor
suggest you do?

CL: Hang in there. And whenever I had a question walk up to them and say, "Hey, I need some help." And I did it for awhile when I got my nerve up, and I would say, "Hey, I need help over here." It was okay for awhile.	Asking for assistance is difficult.

As this client enters into new educational experiences, it will be important for her to have someone with whom to discuss her progress and focus on positive experiences. Assertiveness training or related counseling may be needed so that the client can begin to learn how to take responsibility.

Recreation.   To assess the recreation area, ask your clients what they do with their leisure time. It is important to note whether or not the recreational activities are consistent with their work and educational themes or in contrast with them. This also is a good time to explore love and friendship relations. Exploring clients' social lives within the context of what is done with their leisure time is a relatively nonthreatening way of exploring this sometimes sensitive area. There is no intention of gathering intimate information; rather the intention is to discover how social relations themes may reflect themes identified in work and education settings. Do your clients have many friends? Few? Or none? Do your clients make decisions about leisure activities or do they follow the suggestions of others?

In the following portion of the LCA leisure and social activities are explored:

DIALOGUE	THEMES
CO: Now that you're out of high school, what do you do with your leisure time?	
CL: Well, we have horses and most of the time I ride them. I have two horses and I ride each of	Intense interest and commitment.

them two hours a day. So . . .
really, I don't have much time
to do anything else.

CO: Four hours of horseback
riding a day?

CL: Uh-huh, I get up at 6:00 in the
morning and ride till 8:00.
Now I'll have to ride them both
when I get home. I guess I'll
have to cut down to an hour a
piece. But I've got to ride them
during the week, because
they're not worth a darn if I
don't ride them during the
week for the shows on the
weekend.

CO: So you show them on the
weekends.

CL: We go all over and show them.

CO: So that takes up most of your
time?

CL: Yeah, quite a bit of it, and I
got a Doberman pinscher that
I'm trying to train, and he's
about to drive me crazy. Most
of the time I spend with
animals. We did raise
Dobermans. Two years ago we
had thirteen of them and we
sold all of them. Now we only
have one, this little baby.

CO: So most of your time is spent
with your horses and animals.
What about friends?

CL: Most of my friends live in   Friends come to her.
town, they usually come out
and see me. So it's just whoever
comes out and somebody's
usually out there all the time. I
run around with my friends at
night. Our horse shows last till
about 7:30 then I come home
and go to the dances or
whatever parties are going on.

CO: What about weekends?

CL: Well, our shows are on Sunday,   Her mother is important to her.
so I usually spend the whole
day Saturday with Mom. I
don't get to see her too much
during the week. I see her

every once in awhile at night,
but on Saturdays we go
shopping. We go to breakfast
first and then we shop.
Sometimes we go to lunch. My
mom and I are real close.

CO: You feel responsible for her in
a way.

CL: Yeah. Because she's done real
well in spite of having to raise
all us kids. I know my mom is
just a lot of fun, I have more
fun with her than I do most of
my friends.

CO: She's kind of a mother and a   Mom is someone to go back to.
friend?

CL: Yeah, we're real close.

CO: That's good. So you feel that
you have to take care of her
and provide friendship for
her, too? Maybe when you get
out on your own you'll have
more time for yourself. What
do you think you'll do then?

CL: I'll probably move. If I move to   Relationship with mother may
California my sister may want   interfere with moving to where jobs
me to live with her. If I stay   are.
here, I'd probably move to
Columbia or someplace close so
I could run back and forth to
see Mom.

CO: One of the things holding you
back here is your mother.

CL: I guess. She's married and my   Will she be able to leave home?
stepdad works an awful lot and
I hate for her to be by herself
all the time. I just enjoy seeing
her and I'm kind of used to it,
I guess.

It is relatively simple to move from leisure activities to social relation-ships. In the above example the client's dependency on her animals and her mother for emotional support may interfere with career exploration. This conflict may have to be faced in later individual or group counseling.

Typical Day

Many of the themes that emerge during the LCA have natural oppo-sites, such as active-passive and outgoing-withdrawn. Each of these opposite pairs can be considered a personality dimension. There are at least two personality dimensions that should be examined during the typical day portion of the LCA. These are dependent-independent and spontaneous-systematic.

Dependent-Independent

- Relies on others
- Insists on someone else making decisions

Spontaneous-Systematic

- Stable routine
- Persistent and attentive

The purpose of the typical day exploration is to discover how persons organize their lives. This assessment can be done by asking your clients to describe a typical day in a step-by-step fashion. The dependence-independence dimension can be explored by asking: "Do you get yourself up in the morning or rely on someone else to wake you?" "Do you do things alone or insist on having someone with you at all times?" Similarly, you need to determine whether your clients organize their lives systematically or respond to each day spontaneously? For example, systematic individuals tend to do the same thing day after day in a fairly stable routine (for example, eating raisin bran cereal every morning), while spontaneous individuals rarely do the same thing twice.

An understanding of the patterns that emerge from the typical day assessment can be very helpful to clients, for it is these patterns that often cause problems in school, training, or on the job. For example, if a client confides that he enjoys sleeping late, problems may be foreseen with punctuality and attendance on the job. This should be explored in later career counseling sessions. Again, these patterns should be repeated, clarified, and reflected so that clients begin to gain a clearer understanding of how they organize and carry out their lives.

The following is a portion of the LCA in which a client's typical day is discussed. Notice that the client and counselor explore activities that are common to all people, such as eating and sleeping, as well as those that are more unique to this particular client.

DIALOGUE	THEMES
CO: I'd just like you to think for a minute, what a day would be like for you, a typical day, kind of what you do. It's time to get up. Does an alarm get you up, does somebody wake you up, or do you just wake up?	

CL: I wake up myself. Get up, go downstairs. I've already taken my shower the night before, so I just wash up my face, put on a little make-up, find something to put on, get dressed, fix myself something to eat. Drink lots of milk because my stomach is upset when I get up. I have an ulcer.

Responsible, systematic.

CO: You fix your own breakfast?

CL: Yeah. Eggs or toast . . . then the phone usually rings and I talk.

But dependent.

CO: Who's calling you?

CL: One of my girlfriends.

CO: Let's say you got up and you didn't have anything to do. You could do anything you wanted to do. What would take place?

CL: You want to know what I'd do? Grab a blanket, go downstairs, get something to eat, turn on the TV; just sit there and watch TV.

Passive, seeks pleasure in immediate environment.

CO: You like TV?

CL: Uh-huh.

CO: Daytime TV? Nightime TV?

CL: It depends, I like three soap operas. At night I really don't like TV that much unless it's really a good show or a movie. Other than that I don't watch too much, unless I really like it.

CO: What do you like about soap operas?

CL: Just the story itself, um, the suspense of what's going to happen next. Who's gonna find out what? And, um, who's getting married and who's daughter's pregnant (laughter).

Social interests.

CO: Do you ever . . . can you ever put yourself in their place? Do you ever think that it's happening to you?

CL: I get so mad that I stomp my feet, saying, "Stop! Stop!" or

Identifies with and relates to others easily.

crying, I end up crying. And I
get so mad. You see somebody
behind a curtain with a gun
and you're saying don't go that
way, don't go that way! Call the
police. It's really exciting.
Sometimes you get so mad and
sometimes you get so happy
you start crying. They are a
mess!

The client indicates that she likes a systematic routine for carrying out
her daily living. However, it sounds as if she is dependent on others and
can get caught up in social relationship problems. She seems passive, and
TV could be a pacifier for her.

Strengths and Obstacles

The strengths/obstacles section of the LCA consists of asking clients
what they believe to be their three main strengths and three main obstacles.

Three Main Strengths

· Resources at own disposal
· What resources do for them

Three Main Obstacles

· Relate to strengths
· Relate to themes

This assessment gives direct information about the problems with
which your clients are dealing and the resources they have at their own
disposal to help them. This is accomplished by asking your clients to look at
the roles they play such as mother, father, learner, or worker, and the skills
they use to carry out those roles. After they name their three strengths, it is
best to probe deeper by asking them what these strengths do for them. For
example, if a client lists persistence as a strength, further probing might
disclose that it is a strength because it makes him or her keep trying.

The same kind of probing and clarification also should be done on
obstacles. For some clients it is easier to come up with problems, perhaps
because of past failure or low self-esteem. It is recommended that for such
clients you should look at their obstacles and strengths together. For example, how can strengths be used to offset obstacles? This may help them start
thinking in light of the abilities, competencies, and skills they already possess.

The following is a portion of the LCA in which strengths and obstacles are pinpointed:

DIALOGUE	THEMES
CO: So what would you say would be some of your main strengths besides liking people?	
CL: Oh, I'm a halfway pretty good typist, especially with a little practice. I can run office machines. I've never had any trouble with any kind of office machine. I'm good over the telephone. I can always keep things pretty well organized. I can get things set up, so that if somebody came into the job they'd know exactly what to do. I always make a list of the things I do every day.	Feels confident of her skills. Uses her social skills on the telephone.
CO: That's good, sounds like that's the type of person a secretary should be. What if you could size up your main weaknesses that you'd like to work on as far as being more employable?	
CL: Well, I probably talk too much. If I get started on something, it's hard for me to get off the subject and I probably do run my mouth too often. Another thing I don't pace my time right. Either I'm done too fast or I'm done not fast enough. I never can get everything to work out just right in an exact time slot like I'd like to. I'd always have things done an hour early, or I won't have them done at all. If I could just get things in a better order.	Must control social needs. Concern for being better organized is really a strength.
CO: Then it's important for you to be organized?	
CL: Uh-huh, I like to be organized. And I don't think that there would be anything else that I would have any trouble with.	

The counselor has reinforced the client's desire to be organized and take responsibility. The need for social contact is well suited for telephone and reception activities. However, other social activities on the job will have to be controlled. This can be discussed in later counseling contacts.

During the strength and obstacle section of the LCA, your client may not be able to respond to your request to list three strengths or three obstacles. In such cases, break down the task into smaller parts by asking him or her to list just one strength or obstacle. After one has been discussed, ask for another. This approach takes the pressure off the client to come up with a quick list of things and allows time to come up with more details.

You also may encounter clients who give short answers or answers that contain little information in response to the strengths and obstacles section. For example, a client may give as a strength "I'm a good worker." This response does not reveal much information. To gain more information, you can ask, "What does being a good worker mean to you?" or "What do you believe are the best things about the way you work?" Vague answers may be encountered in other sections of the LCA. In describing a typical day a client may state "I get up, go to work, come home, eat, and go to bed." Again, little information can be gleaned from this statement. Instead, ask, "How do you wake up? Does an alarm clock wake you or does someone else get you up? How do you get breakfast?" Continue examining the client's day in similar detail.

Another situation to which you should be ready to respond is a client who cannot think of any strengths. One strategy is to simply move on to the obstacles section and then be especially sensitive to strengths that may be hidden. For example, a client who lists as an obstacle "I work too slow" may reveal on further probing, "I pay a lot of attention to detail and want to be sure everything is right." Another strategy is to recall and reflect some of the themes expressed in other parts of the LCA. You might say to the client, "When you were talking about your typical day, you explained that your schedule was different each day depending on the schedule of other people in your family. Yet you seem to be able to get done what you need to each day. It seems to me that you are very flexible and adaptable." Such statements help clients discover strengths they can bring to a job, can result in greater self-esteem, and may stimulate clients to think of other strengths.

One final strategy that you should consider whenever a client seems unwilling to talk freely is to examine your career counseling style. Although even the most skillful helpers encounter clients who do not open up to them, all counselors need to check their use of human relationship skills when their interaction with clients seem to be unproductive. Are you using good attending and listening skills? Good perceiving skills? Are helpful response styles present?

Summary

The summary section is the last portion of the LCA. There are two primary purposes for conducting a summary. One purpose is to emphasize the information that has been gained during the interview. During the summary, it is not necessary to review every bit of information obtained, but prominent life themes, strengths, and obstacles should be repeated. It is helpful if you ask your clients to summarize what they have learned from the session. Having them take the lead in expressing what has been learned increases the impact of the information, thus increasing self-awareness. It also lets you know what your clients have gained and, in some cases, missed. When your clients have finished, you can add any points that seem to have been omitted. It is important that you and your clients reach agreement about their life themes. This agreement is effective particularly when it can be reached using your clients' own words and meanings.

The second major purpose of the summary is to relate the information gained to goals that you and your clients may work toward that will enhance your clients' possible job choices, career exploration, or career planning. The life themes that have been revealed may suggest possible occupational choices that require further exploration, may rule out certain other choices, and may suggest barriers that will need to be overcome. From the strengths and obstacles discovered, positive aspects of your clients may have been revealed that can be developed further. Then, too, weaknesses that need to be overcome also may be apparent, in which case you and your client can decide to establish goals and form plans of action to reach these goals.

The following example is a summary of an LCA interview. Notice that the counselor attempts to highlight important life career themes, skills, competencies, and obstacles; allows the client to express what has been learned; attempts to reach agreement with the client on the client's life career themes and skills using the client's own words; and relates the information gained to goals and possible courses of action.

CO: Pam, we've been talking for several minutes here and I guess I wanted to bring this altogether for you and look at what we have talked about. What do you see yourself learning from today? What is it that we have taught you about yourself, maybe that you weren't looking at before?

CL: Well, I'm not real sure.

CO: Look back at when we talked about your daily routines, doing the same things, being organized, what would you see that telling about yourself as far as your abilities.

CL: Well, I guess I'm organized. I guess I'm kind of responsible.

CO: Responsible in what way?

CL: I'm real concerned for Jill. I do want to raise her well. My mom is always giving me a hard time about making sure to bring her up right. So, I think I am responsible with her.

CO: When we talked about your strengths, we came up with things like you were very dependable, we talked about that you hadn't missed very many days at work, that you are really conscious about getting to work on time, not being absent, that kind of thing. From your typical day it sounds like you are very organized and have things at hand as to what you're going to do and I get the feeling that you are responsible, too. How do you see that working to your advantage in this program?

CL: Well, I think it will be useful for me especially in my work experience, at the law office, you know, I think that I am going to be able to handle some of the things that they give me to do there.

CO: Chance to apply some of the skills you have.

CL: I've really enjoyed the typing that they give me to do there, but I'm still kind of scared about whether I'm going to be able to pass the GED.

CO: I can understand your concern about that. It is a big step. Sounds like the diploma is important to you since you didn't get a chance to graduate.

CL: Yeah, it is. I think if I'm going to go on and become a legal secretary maybe, I think I would need my GED.

CO: Well, I think we've got a good start here today. Some of the concerns maybe that you are worried about are passing your GED and being ready for the test. We can work on it and the next time we meet we can start setting up some things for us to do. Okay?

ADDING THE FAMILY ROLE TO THE LCA

The LCA is designed to cover your clients' level of functioning in various life roles including the worker, learner, and personal roles as well as yielding information on how they negotiate with their environment. As you use the LCA you may wish to add other life-roles to the career assessment process. One life-role that you may wish to add is the family role.

There are a number of techniques that can be used to add the family role to the LCA. Dickson and Parmerlee (1980) describe the use of the occupational family tree, which consists of a one-page worksheet on which responders list the following:

1. Occupations of their grandparents
2. Occupations of their parents
3. Occupations of their aunts and uncles
4. Occupations of their brothers and sisters
5. Responder's preferred choice

Family members with whom the responder has a close relationship are circled. An asterisk is placed next to those who are admired but there is no close relationship. Finally, the occupation that appears to be the one preferred by the family for the respondent is identified.

An assignment can be provided for writing responses in advance of the use of the LCA. Items for the assignment include (Dickson and Parmerlee, 1980, pp. 102–103):

1. How do you feel about the occupations of your relatives (proud, embarrassed)?

2. On what basis do you feel they want you to select the specified occupation (statement, hints, threats)?

3. Do your present occupational interests fit both your abilities and the need for such workers (aptitudes, job trends)?

4. List several low-class (low pay or low prestige) jobs/careers that have some positive stereotypes (bus driver, hospital aide).

5. List several high-class (high pay or high prestige) jobs/careers that have some negative stereotypes (car dealer, attorney).

6. What are the satisfactions from occupations my family has enjoyed most (leisure time, travel, living conditions)?

7. Which family member am I most alike (characteristics, interests, abilities)?

8. What personal work habits or characteristics have made my family successful/satisfied and unsuccessful/dissatisfied on the job?

Career Genograms

Genograms (Bowen, 1978; Guerin and Pendagast, 1976) have been used extensively by counselors who work with families in family counseling. Their basic format can be adapted for use in the LCA. The addition of this technique to the LCA will aid you in understanding client information from the broader perspective of family structure dynamics. For example, it may help you understand better the work adjustment problems and skill training learning problems clients may have as well as their preferred work environments.

The introduction of the occupational family tree or the career genogram to the LCA changes the focus of the LCA as well as the way you work with clients during the LCA process. Both require paper and pencil or a chalk board. The career genogram, in particular, require a place for you to draw family relationships. The use of these techniques also will add to the time it takes to complete the LCA. This is especially true if you decide to use the career genogram. However, the time used may be well spent because it can help shed light on issues or concerns that may surface only because of a focus on the family structure and family dynamics.

We recommend that if family structure and dynamics information appears to be useful in career counseling using the LCA that you assess this life-role arena after you have completed the typical day or the strengths and obstacles section of the LCA. Although the career genogram technique is longer and takes more time to complete, it yields more information. If time is of concern, the career genogram can be completed in a second session after you have used the LCA.

If you decide to use the career genogram, we suggest that you introduce its use by telling clients that this technique helps you add to your knowledge and understanding about them and their families, particularly as this information relates to their functioning in other life roles. You might say something like, "This next section of the LCA will help us understand you and your family better. We will be drawing a picture of your family as we talk." What follows are the guiding questions that you can use to conduct the career genogram.

A. *Introduction*
This next section of the LCA will help us understand you and your family better. We will be drawing a picture of your family as we talk.

B. *Guiding Questions*
1. Courtship stage
    a. Length of courtship?
    b. What attracted you to each other?
    c. How much time did you spend together as a couple and how was this decided? (Probe into who pursued for more togetherness and time apart in the relationship).
    d. When your relationship became exclusive, how did you handle your individual friendships?
    e. How did your parents view your relationship?
    f. Any previous marriages? Children from these marriages?

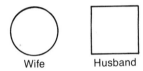

2. Marriage before children
    a. What prompted you to get married at the time you did?
    b. How would you describe your relationship during this time?
    c. Amount and nature of individual time and time with friends?
    d. Life-style: Social, financial, educational, time spent with in-laws?

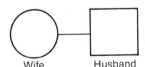

3. Family with children
    a. What entered into your decision to have a child when you did?
    b. How did marital relationship change with birth of child?
    c. How did your individual roles change?
    d. Describe each child for me (oldest to youngest). May use Adlerian rating format to supplement.
    e. Who takes care of whom, plays with whom, fights/argues the most, is the most different, is the most alike?

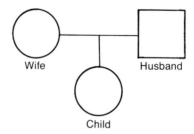

4. Family with child referred for counseling
   a. Are there any significant events in the birth/development? (Probe pregnancy experience.)
   b. What kind of child was he/she?
   c. What have been your concerns? When did you first become concerned?
   d. What have you done about your concerns? How have you been dealing with them?
   e. What are your feelings at the present time? What are your expectations?

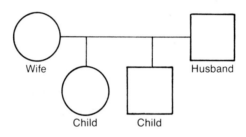

5. Extended family
   a. How would you describe the family in which you grew up?
   b. What is your father's occupation? What is your mother's occupation? (Probe: Other work experience? Education or training? Satisfaction with their careers, unfulfilled dreams?)
   c. Probe: What is/was your mother like; father like; adjective to describe; nature of marital relationship (responsibilities).
   d. What are the occupations of your brothers and/or sisters? For younger siblings, what do they aspire to be? Where do your brothers and sisters live? Describe the life-style of each. Probe: If the family lives close by, explore cousin relationships (such as competitiveness for grandparent's approval).
   e. What is your role in the family (present and when growing up)?
   f. What is your relationship with your mother, father? Probe: career aspirations for you; cohesiveness.
   g. Who are you most like in your family? Probe: who took care of whom: coalitions.
   h. What is your spouse's relationship with your family?

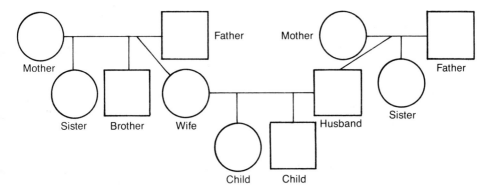

6. Describe a typical day
   a. Take a specific week day within the last seven days and describe the events from morning to night.
   b. Describe a specific weekend day—how it differs.
      Interviewer probe: chores, couple time apart from children, family time, time with siblings, peer time for children.
7. This "task" provides information regarding structural characteristics and task efficiency of the family. Tool can be used alone for a quick assessment of the family structure. Include children if these are available.
   Family Tasks
   Instructions given to family (interviewer does not enter into discussion):
   a. Family is to define one small family problem. They are not to attempt to solve it (ten minutes).
   b. Family is to discuss their family life in five to ten years from now (ten minutes). How will it be? How would they like it to be.
   The family tasks create a situation in which family members are required to interact directly with each other toward a common goal. The family is actually acting out its dynamics rather than simply talking about how they function as a family.
   Depending on the setting in which the assessment is being done, other tasks of more appropriate content may be used. For example, if the parents are concerned about their adolescent's future, an appropriate task would be for the family to define a career goal they wish their adolescent to attain. The interviewer should not intervene during the tasks portion, even if the family attempts to include him or her, as this will alter the family interaction patterns.
C. *Summary*
   1. Questions from family
   2. Interviewer may wish to summarize family strengths and areas for growth
   3. Closing statements regarding how the information will be processed

Dagley (1984) suggests another set of questions to be used in developing a career genogram.

- What are the dominant values in the family of origins?
- Vocationally, are certain "missions" valued?
- Are there any "ghosts or legends" which serve either as anchor points or "rightful roles" for the family?
- What myths or misconceptions seem to transcend generations?
- Are there any psychological pressures or expectations emanating from "unfinished business" of the family?
- How does the individual's description of economic values and preferences fit in with family's history?
- How has the family addressed the three boxes of life (learning, working, and playing)? Any imbalances?
- What family interaction rules and relationship boundaries have been passed along through generations?
- Are there any voids in the client's memory of family? Any significance to those voids?
- Does the client have a sense of "owing" family traditions? What are the accrued debits and credits?
- How have the primary life tasks of love, work, and friendship been addressed by the family?
- What vocational patterns emerge, in terms of choices, as well as the choice and development process?

To use the career genogram effectively, you will need to learn the following genogram symbols:

Couple Symbols:

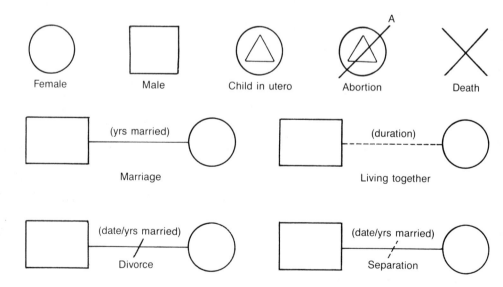

Name/Age/Duration:

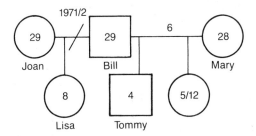

Dagley (1984) summed up the use of the career genogram by suggesting that an intergenerational approach has special utility in both career counseling and marriage and family counseling. The simple premise underlying this approach is that counselors have a greater opportunity to be helpful if they understand their clients. Family mapping can enhance the indepth understanding of a client by providing perspective. Indeed, the achievement of accurate empathic understanding requires a contextual conceptualization of the client's phenomenological world. A family history interview can yield substance crucial to the understanding of a particular behavior or dilemma. Career-choice conflicts often can best be understood in the context of a person's sociological, psychological, and economic heritage. The same is true with other conflicts such as marital relationship difficulties and family interaction conflicts.

In summary, it is necessary to be clear about the purpose of a career genogram, which is to obtain a graphic picture of a person's career heritage. Specific attention should be given to identification of (1) occupations represented in a three- to four-generation family tree, (2) status and value rankings typically assigned occupations by various family members, (3) career choice patterns or ways in which family members have selected or changed occupations, (4) economic expectations or pressures, and (5) family work values. It also may be of value to determine the peer group context in which the person grew up (Dagley, 1984).

SOME CLOSING THOUGHTS

Using Transitions

The LCA will be most effective if you use a conversational, somewhat casual voice tone. One way to help ensure that a conversational atmosphere is maintained is to use transitional statements. A transition is a statement by you that signals to clients that the focus or topic of the interview is going to be changed. By using transition sentences, you let clients know that the topic is being changed and what the new topic is.

One way you can accomplish smooth transitions from one section of the LCA to another is to pay attention to wording. Make the first part of your statement a brief response to something your client has said in the last section, the second part of your statement is an introduction to the next topic: "Well, it seems that working has been enjoyable for you and you see it as valuable. Did you have these same feelings about being in school, or did you have different outlook there?"

Another helpful strategy is to avoid long introductions to a new area that will break the conversational tone: "Okay, we've talked about work and school and about how you spend your free time. I'd like to shift now and ask you to describe your typical day." In this example the counselor does not have a good tie-in between the areas but briefly describes the areas covered, signals to the client that a change in focus is coming, and lets the client know what the new topic is, all using a minimum of words.

At what points in the LCA are transitions likely to be needed? Usually transition statements will be needed whenever you wish to move from one major section of the LCA such as the typical day to another such as strengths and obstacles. Transitions also will be helpful when moving from one area to another within a major section, such as between work experience, education or training, and recreation.

Adapting the LCA for Younger Clients

The goals for using the LCA with younger clients may differ markedly from those for older, more mature clients. For example, older clients may possess a higher level of career maturity and be in need of help in acclimating to a specific work setting, remediation of past inappropriate work habits, or expanding their career options. As younger clients' experiences are generally more limited, your goals may include such items as introducing the world of work, appropriate work habits, and beginning to explore a variety of occupations as a prerequisite to occupational choice.

The LCA can be adapted easily for younger clients. These adaptations are listed by LCA section as follows:

Career Assessment

Work Experience. It is probable that younger clients have not had paid work experience. Many young people perform tasks around home, however, and these can be used in the same way that jobs are used with adults. Domestic responsibilities such as mowing the lawn, caring for a younger brother or sister, or doing the dishes are examples of these tasks.

Educational Experience. This is an important area to cover with younger clients and should be done in essentially the same manner as with older clients. Special emphasis should be placed on teachers, counselors, and administrators that younger clients liked or disliked and why. This provides information regarding the types of persons they respect or tend to emulate or have difficulty cooperating with. Subject matter preferences also are important considerations to help explore later job placement possibilities and possible occupational interests and to help determine future school subject choices related to an eventual occupation choice.

Recreation. The area of recreation can be examined in terms of family recreational activities. It may be of interest to look at what kind of family activities are undertaken to obtain an idea of family ties. Another area to explore is hobbies. Do your younger clients enjoy activities such as stamp collecting or more adventurous endeavors such as skateboarding or exploring? Ask them to describe a best friend or friends to help determine the kind of peer influence that exists.

Typical Day

The typical day section can be explored in much the same way as it is for older clients. Again, you are looking for independent-dependent, systematic-spontaneous tendencies. Who gets younger clients up in the morning? Do they have a set schedule? Do they have daily chores? If so, are responsibilities monitored? Are privileges contingent on fulfilling responsibilities? What is the home environment like?

Strengths and Obstacles

This section also is done much the same as it is for older clients. The focus is on recognizing strengths used to overcome obstacles. By having their strengths reinforced, clients may become more cognizant of the skills they possess.

Summary

The summary is done by asking younger clients what they learned from the session. It is important to instill an awareness of likes and dislikes and to organize strengths and obstacles to show how these come together in an overall method of operation or life-style. For example, do younger clients like teachers because they give encouragement? This may indicate a need for reinforcement in order to carry out tasks most efficiently. Such points are important revelations that can have implications for future occupational and personal success.

Applying What Has Been Learned

The LCA is a structured interview technique designed to help you and your clients gather information in a systematic way in a relatively short period of time. Please note the words *structured interview*. We see the LCA as just that, a structured interview. As such the LCA is a point of departure for the next steps in career counseling, because it helps to form positive relationships with clients from which future career counseling activities can take place.

The structure of the LCA provides stimuli, which in turn evoke client responses. You acknowledge and dignify those responses by helping your clients identify and describe their responses in theme form. Together, you apply that knowledge to possible next steps such as testing, counseling, educational and occupational information gathering, and career planning and decision making.

The LCA is particularly useful as a preliminary step to test taking and test interpretation. Briggs and Keller state that clients need to be involved in all phases of testing including orientation, test use, and test interpretation. They put it this way:

> To use test information effectively in counseling, clients need to have a rationale for using tests and a high degree of involvement in the decision making regarding the use and the interpretation of the tests. They must also be taught to use test information to make observations, inferences, and hypotheses about themselves and their future courses of action. (Briggs and Keller, 1982, p. 531)

You will find that as you use the LCA, it sets the stage for test taking and test interpretation, because the process used in the LCA teaches clients beginning skills in making observations, inferences, and hypotheses about themselves through life career theme identification. These beginning skills can have direct carryover since the language used to identify and describe client life career themes is the same language often used in test interpretation. An example of this is the use of Holland codes to interpret the Strong-Campbell Interest Inventory (SCII).

As you use the LCA you also will find that it sets the stage for career counseling. It provides a comfortable, nonthreatening way to begin to bring issues and concerns requiring career counseling attention to the surface. The LCA also will bring to the surface the ways clients gather and process information about themselves and the world in which they live. The styles they use may have implications for the kind of career counseling you do in helping them learn how to gather and process career information and make informed decisions based on that information (Johnson, 1978).

The LCA supports and reinforces a holistic approach to career counseling. It helps begin a discussion of the life-role arenas of worker, learner, personal, and possible family and their relationships. This is important in career counseling because, as Berman and Munson point out

> Significant career involvements do not exist in isolation of, nor can they be understood apart from, other life ventures. People can be helped to identify areas of meaningful individual-environment dialogue and to examine their worklife experiences in conjunction with family, community, school, and other important roles. (Berman and Munson, 1981, p. 96)

REFERENCES

BERMAN, J. J., and MUNSON, H. L., "Challenges in a Dialectical Conception of Career Evolution," *The Personnel and Guidance Journal*, 60, no. 2 (1981).
BOWEN, M., *Family Therapy in Clinical Practice.* New York: Jason Aronson, 1978.
BRIGGS, D. A., and KELLER, K. A., "A Cognitive Approach to Using Tests in Counseling," *The Personnel and Guidance Journal*, 60, no. 9 (1982).
DAGLEY, J., "A Vocational Genogram" (mimeograph), Athens: University of Georgia, 1984.
DICKSON, G. L., and PARMERLEE, J. R., "The Occupational Family Tree: A Career Counseling Technique," *The School Counselor* 28, no. 2 (1980).
DINKMEYER, D. C., PEW, W. L., and DINKMEYER, D. C., *Adlerian Counseling and Psychotherapy.* Monterey, Calif.: Brooks/Cole, 1979.
GUERIN, P. J., JR., and PENDAGAST, E. G., "Evaluation of Family System and Genogram," in *Family Therapy: Theory and Practice*, ed. P. J. Guerin, Jr. New York: Gardner, 1976.
JOHNSON, R. H., "Individual Styles of Decision Making: A Theoretical Model for Counseling," *The Personnel and Guidance Journal*, 56, no. 9, (1978).
MOSAK, H. H., "Lifestyle," in *Techniques for Behavior Change*, ed. A. G. Nikelly. Springfield, Ill.: Charles C Thomas, 1971.

CHAPTER 4

Personal Styles Analysis

JOSEPH T. KUNCE and CORRINE S. COPE

Life-style concepts are becoming increasingly relevant for contemporary career development theory and practice. A life-span perspective of careers requires consideration of concepts such as roles, tasks, transitions, and stages. Watkins (1984), for example, delineates the career applications of life-styles and roles according to Adler's concepts of individual psychology. In a similar way Keirsey and Bates (1978) discuss the use of the Myers-Briggs type indicator in vocational decision making. Life-style constructs also have been found useful in describing a wide range of behaviors from cognitive, learner, and teacher styles (Kirby, 1979) to interpersonal interactions as interpreted by transactional analysis (Woollams and Brown, 1979).

The concept of life-styles or personality types is not new. Centuries ago Hippocrates proposed the existence of basic personality types. More recently, Jung (1923) hypothesized psychological types based on one's behavioral preferences in responding to one's environment. Adler (1956) used the construct of styles in his explanation of individual psychology. Currently, Holland's (1985) concepts of basic types in both personality and occupations are widely accepted and used in career counseling.

The construct of life-style or personality type is based on the theory

Joseph T. Kunce is professor and Corrine S. Cope is professor emeritus in the Department of Educational and Counseling Psychology at the University of Missouri–Columbia.

that one develops preferred ways of responding to one's environment. These preferences develop into habits, interests, and skills during normal growth. An important concept in life-style theory is that no preferred way of behaving is right or wrong; the preferences developed by one person are no more or less desirable than those developed by another. Self-understanding resulting from knowledge about one's own personal style should be helpful in career planning and decision making and in dealing with other events and relationships in one's life.

The grouping of behaviors into personality types is an attempt to organize the complexities of human behavior into a manageable and understandable system. A major problem in life-style or personality type theory is determination of the specific dimensions that differentiate types and the labeling of those dimensions. Some life-style theories, such as those of Adler (1956) and Merrill and Reid (1981), identify four basic styles. The Myers-Briggs type indicator (Myers, 1975), based on Jungian theory, delineates four pairs of opposite personality types. Use of a minimum of personality types aids understanding but may tend to make human behavior appear too simplistic. The categories are global, and important individual differences may not be accounted for. Previous work by Kunce (1979) suggests that personal style descriptions should account for differences in at least three major areas—emotional, physical, and cognitive—with specific dimensions in each of these areas.

In this chapter we describe a personal styles model and its uses in career assessment and counseling. The format for the chapter is (1) a presentation of the rationale for using life-styles as a meaningful way of describing human behavior; (2) a description of a personal styles model; (3) instructions on how to use the model as an assessment tool, and (4) illustrations of how clients can use the obtained information to choose career pathways more compatible with their unique life-styles and to cope more effectively in their everyday lives.

The basic purpose of our model is to demonstrate that personality can be described in terms of adaptive life-styles that are useful in understanding career development. We provide and carefully document a conceptual framework for the analysis of significant and basic predispositions that provide substance and shape to a client's life-style. In this model we delineate an interrelated set of personal styles for each of three modes of expression: emotional, physical, and cognitive. Systematic assessment of these characteristics provides a practical procedure for enabling clients to evaluate their unique pattern of styles in meaningful relationship to education, training, work, and personal-social environments. The utilization of the model, in effect, becomes a decision-making tool for assisting clients in choosing career pathways in terms of their own particular constellation of personal styles.

PERSONAL STYLES RATIONALE

Four basic assumptions underlie our personal styles model. These assumptions are (1) personal styles represent characteristic not transitory modes of self-expression; (2) personal styles can be subdivided into more basic bipolar subtypes that are interrelated in a circumplex format; (3) there are universally recognized and basic personality styles identifiable among existing theories of personality; and (4) personality style specificity is facilitated by identifying more than one mode of personal expression for circumplex description.

Personal Styles Definition

A personal style represents a characteristic manner of personal expression that is analogous to a personality trait. A style is distinguishable from a transitory personal reaction or personality state. Extroversion-introversion conceptualizations, for example, invariably imply that any one person's style can be characterized more accurately either by an extroversion or by an introversion definition. This characterization tends to be as predictable of one's future behavior under specified environmental conditions (such as one's style of performing in front of a large audience) as of behavior at the time of assessment. In contrast, assessments of levels of anxiety, depression, hostility, and confusion are generally designed to provide an accurate measurement of the person's present emotional state. Such emotional states can be expected to change and consequently may be indicative more of a person's emotional/cognitive reactions to transitory stresses than of enduring behavioral predispositions.

Personal style formulations should have longer term career implications than personality descriptions based on psychological tests that measure a person's emotional, physical, and/or cognitive distress. Furthermore, many popularly used personality tests are designed to diagnose problems of psychological adjustment and customarily include questions that appear irrelevant, intrusive, and even offensive to clients whose primary concerns are career related. Although it may be possible to use scores from a personality test such as the Minnesota Multiphasic Personality Inventory (MMPI) to infer personality styles (Kunce and Anderson, 1976, 1984; Kunce, 1979) and although it may be possible to distinguish between specific state-trait aspects of a characteristic such as anxiety (Spielbarger, Gorsuch, and Lushene, 1970), the use of other assessment techniques and tools may be more satisfactory.

A wide variety of assessment procedures is currently available to relate personal styles in relationship to careers. Holland's conceptualization for typing both a person and the occupation as realistic-investigative-artistic-social-enterprising-conventional has widespread acceptance in career assessment and counseling. The coding of Myers-Briggs personality types of extroversion-introversion, sensing-intuition, thinking-feeling, and judgment-perception and relating them to careers is a similar technique. Life history inventories that assess preferences for and engagement in educational, work, and social activities also serve as a means for uncovering personal styles or themes that have career significance.

Distinguishing between personal styles and transitory emotional/physical/cognitive reactions is an important differentiation to make in career assessment and counseling. Analysis of personal styles will enable clients to understand the role that personality has in adjusting to the roles and functions demanded from their present and anticipated social and occupational environments. This understanding should also encourage clients to think in terms of long-term career satisfaction and satisfactoriness. Concurrently, effective counseling necessitates acknowledgment of the more immediate effects of the personality states of anxiety, depression, and confusion and current stressors such as family and finances on short-term and more immediate career decisions.

Circumplex Formulations for Personal Style Description

Leary (1957) proposed defining personal styles in terms of a circumplex model of personality, which he named the interpersonal behavior circle. He plotted in circular form a series of interpersonal behavior styles defined by the magnitude of a person's need for love and for dominance. The circular arrangement permits description of pairs of opposite personal styles (Fig. 4–1). For example, high dominance with low need for love describes a competitive person, and low dominance with high need for love, a docile person. Variations of this kind of personality type formulations are widespread. A personality inventory developed by Krug (1984) depicts diagrammatically eight interpersonal styles in octagonal fashion. Merrill and Reid (1981) use a fourplex model defined by two factors, emotional responsiveness and assertiveness. Their model yields four personality types with diagonal pairs representing opposite types: analytic versus expressive and driving versus amiable (Fig. 4–2).

Personality typing by Leary, Krug, and Merrill and Reid permits advantageous circular, or "circumplex," arrangement of two or more bipolar psychological factors into behaviorally meaningful association. Such arrangements also provide a means of perceiving the similarity among personality types hypothesized by a wide variety of personality theorists. Leary's interpersonal circle, for example, can be seen as an extension of personality types proposed by Hippocrates. Hippocrates' four basic personality types of sanguine, melancholic, choloric, and phlegmatic show similarity to the two pairs of opposite types in Leary's circumplex model.

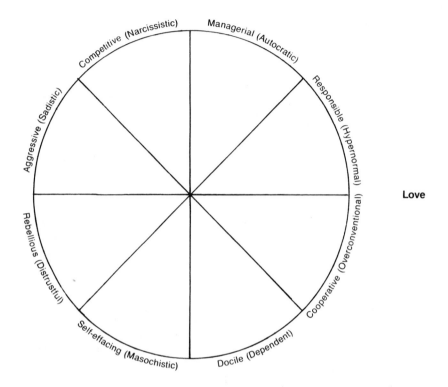

FIGURE 4–1   A circumplex description of personality styles: The interpersonal behavior circle. (The words in parentheses represent the pathological extremes of the personality styles.) (Adapted from T. Leary, *Interpersonal Diagnosis of Personality: A Function Theory and Methodology for Personality Evaluation.* Copyright © Timothy Leary, 1957. Used with permission.)

The sanguine and melancholic types could be placed to coincide, respectively, with Leary's managerial and self-effacing "opposites"; and the choloric and phlegmatic types to coincide with the aggressive and cooperative opposites.

Basic Emotional Styles

In the construction of our personal styles model we assume that there are universal, recognized basic personal styles. To support this assumption we developed a circumplex model based on our research and empirical observations that describe eight interrelated styles of emotional expressiveness. These eight styles represent four bipolar dimensions for emotional expressiveness: zestful versus reserved, expansive versus modest, confrontive versus patient, and empathic versus restive. Table 4–1 provides our definitions for each of the eight emotional styles. In developing our terms and definitions we tried to avoid the "psychopathology error" of describing behavior in a negative or derogatory manner. We believe it is important for counselors working with clients to have a repertoire of positive, constructive words to describe coping behaviors.

The interconnectedness of styles is illustrated in Fig. 4–3. For each basic style in this model, there is an opposite style as well as two closely related styles. The circular arrangement depicts zestful and reserved, expansive and modest, confrontive and patient, and restive and empathic at opposite ends of four dimensions of emotional expressiveness. Furthermore, each style is similar to those adjacent to it in the circle, for example, zestful with empathic and expansive.

The existence of universally recognized types of personal styles can be illustrated via the "fit" of various personality types with our proposed circumplex model of emotional expressiveness. Table 4–2 schematically presents the relationship of these eight styles of emotional expressiveness

Analytical	Driver
Slow reaction Maximum effort to organize Minimum concern for relationships Historical time frame Cautious action Tends to reject involvement	Swift reaction Maximum effort to control Minimum concern for caution in relationships Present time frame Direct action Tends to reject inaction
Unhurried reaction Maximum effort to relate Minimum concern for effecting change Present time frame Supportive action Tends to reject conflict	Rapid reaction Maximum effort to involve Minimum concern for routine Future time frame Impulsive action Tends to reject isolation
Amiable	Expressive

FIGURE 4–2   A fourplex description of personality styles. (Adapted from D. W. Merrill and R. H. Reid, *Personal Styles and Effective Performance* [Radnor, Pa.: Chilton, 1981]. Used with permission.)

TABLE 4–1   Emotional Styles Definitions

Zestful	Shows an enthusiastic and optimistic disposition, emphasizing the positive rather than negative aspects of events.
Expansive	Shows an energetic and forceful disposition, enjoying performing and debating in front of others.
Confrontive	Shows a volatile and changeable disposition, demonstrating straightforwardly one's own internal mood or emotional state.
Restive	Shows an intense and urgent disposition, becoming openly annoyed and irritable when confronted by frustrating situations.
Reserved	Shows a concerned and sensitive disposition, being self-conscious in expressing feelings in public situations.
Modest	Shows a moderate and humble self-esteem, being free of vanity and boastfulness.
Patient	Shows a considerate and calm disposition, restraining one's own feelings to avoid offending others.
Empathic	Shows a sympathetic and understanding disposition, responding easily in concert with emotions of others.

Source: J. T. Kunce, C. S. Cope, and R. M. Newton, *Manual for the Personal Styles Analysis* (Columbia, Mo.: Educational and Psychological Consultants, 1986).

to conceptualizations of a selective sample of personality types delineated by others.

From a study of Table 4–2 it can be seen that a number of personality types closely correspond to our adjective labels. Note the following types associated with *expansive,* sociable, dominant, expressive, and gamesman; with *restive,* hostile, aggressive, driver, and jungle fighter; with *modest,* withdrawn, self-effacing, analytical, and craftsman; and with *empathic,* caring, cooperative, amiable, and company man.

Personal Styles Modes

A major limitation of most systems that describe personality types and styles lies in their lack of specificity, yet their popularity lies in their simplicity for categorizing behavior. This simplicity can lead to uncritical acceptance of overly encompassing definitions. Defining oneself according to such concepts as type A or type B behavior, zodiac signs, extrovert-introvert, neurotic-sociopathic-psychotic, and so on, finds widespread appeal and acceptance. This uncritical acceptance of superficial descriptions has been termed the Barnum effect (O'Dell, 1972; Snyder, Shenkel, and Lowrey, 1977). The same simplicity engenders rejection of the validity of personal style formulations by more critical or informed persons.

Greater precision in personal styles analysis can be achieved by subdividing styles into more discrete categories and by increasing the number of circumplexes to represent more than one behavioral domain. The circumplex model for emotional styles proposed in Fig. 4–3 contains eight personal styles as contrasted to Merrill and Reid's four types. The addition of

TABLE 4–2 Emotional Styles Similarities

KUNCE, COPE, & NEWTON (1986)	KRUG (1984)	LEARY (1957)	ADLER (1956)	MERRILL & REID (1981)	MACCOBY (1976)	HIPPOCRATES
Zestful	Assertive	Responsible	Useful	—	—	Sanguine
Expansive	Sociable	Dominant	—	Expressive	Gamesman	—
Confrontive	Rebellious	Competitive	Ruling	—	—	Choleric
Restive	Hostile	Aggressive	—	Driver	Jungle-fighter	—
Reserved	Submissive	Distrustful	Avoiding	—	—	Melancholic
Modest	Withdrawn	Self-effacing	—	Analytical	Craftsman	—
Patient	Adapting	Docile	Getting	—	—	Phlegmatic
Empathic	Caring	Cooperative	—	Amiable	Company man	—

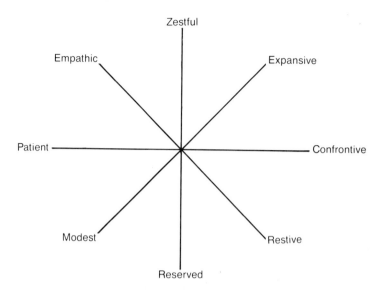

FIGURE 4–3   Basic emotional styles. (Adapted from J. T. Kunce, C. S. Cope, and R. M. Newton, *Manual for the Personal Styles Analysis* [Columbia, Mo.: Educational and Psychological Consultants, 1986].)

other behavioral domains, such as cognitive, that could be similarly subdivided in circumplex fashion would exponentially increase the flexibility for describing behavior. The circumplex in Fig. 4–3 contains four bipolar factors: zestful-reserved, expansive-modest, and so on, making possible 2^4, or 16, combinations of terms. The addition of a second circumplex with four bipolar factors would make possible 2^8, or 256, combinations of terms. Finer subdivisions within a circumplex or adding additional circumplexes therefore can lead to relatively precise definitions of personal styles. These descriptions can be useful in understanding human behavior and interpersonal interactions.

The personality assessment system (PAS) is one of the few existing systems that subdivide personality types in each of several behavioral domains or modes (Gittinger, 1964; Krauskopf and Davis, 1969). This system uses patterns of IQ subtest scores to define personal styles. The three behavioral domains identified are a social mode, a procedural mode, and an intellectual mode. Each mode can be divided into a number of subtypes. Table 4–3 presents a simplified fourplex version of the PAS model for each of the three modes. The PAS model permits a highly complex basis for describing personality, with subtypes further defined from a developmental perspective in terms of primitive, basic, and surface levels of behavior.

Considerable evidence exists to establish a need for addressing a minimum of three behavioral modes—emotional, physical, and cognitive—to adequately assess personal styles. In addition to PAS research, independent analyses of MMPI personality data on a stratified sample of normal and distressed clients (Kunce and Tamkin, 1981) and MMPI group profiles of psychiatric patients categorized by diagnostic types (Skinner and Jackson, 1978) produced three similar orthogonal behavior domains. Kunce terms the three personality dimensions as bipolar factors: self-confident versus self-reliant, empathic versus adventurous, and imaginative versus focused. Counterpart terms for maladaptive behavior on the same factors are sociopathic versus withdrawn, neurotic versus manic, and psychotic versus dogmatic. Skinner and Jackson's comparable dimensions are presented as psychopathological unipolar traits termed sociopathic, neurotic, and psychotic. Conceptually, these analyses appear to provide data that relate to

TABLE 4-3 PAS Concepts

I. *Social (A-U) Mode*
Uncompensated *role uniform:*
Plays uniform social role

Uncompensated *role adaptive:*
Spontaneous, versatile role player

Compensated *role adaptive:*
Rejects role versatility as a
basis of acceptance

Compensated *role uniform:*
Consciously learns a variety of
roles

II. *Procedural (R-F) Mode*
Uncompensated *flexible:*
Admires and respects protocol
but must understand purpose

Uncompensated *regulated:* Natural
dependence on procedures but
needs external discipline

Compensated *regulated:*
Demands flexibility, interested
in procedures

Compensated *flexible:* Likes to
develop own procedures;
argumentative, stubborn

III. *Intellectual (E-I) Mode*
Uncompensated *externalizer:*
Emphasizes relationship

Uncompensated *internalizer:*
Creative and imaginative

Compensated *internalizer:*
Ideas must be useful

Compensated *externalizer:*
Responds selectively to ideational
and idealistic aspects

Source: Adapted from C. Krauskopf and K. Davis, *Studies of the Normal Personality* (Columbia, Mo.: University of Missouri–Columbia Testing and Counseling Service, 1969), pp. 112–16.

the same underlying behavior domains. Krug (1984) also establishes three behavior domains for personality assessment. His test provides scores grouped into three areas: eight interpersonal styles presented in circumplex fashion, seven personal characteristics, and six career life-style factors. Considerable evidence thus exists that a personal styles model must assess several behavior domains to avoid overly simplified descriptions of behavior.

A PERSONAL STYLES MODEL

Our personal styles model in its present form permits assessment of a total of twenty-four life-styles within three discrete behavior domains: emotional, physical, and cognitive. This holistic approach of describing behavior permits a comprehensive overview of critical facets of human dispositions.

We have described in a previous section eight styles of *emotional* expression: zestful, expansive, confrontive, restive, and so on. Using similar procedures we developed eight key words and accompanying definitions to describe a person's physical *behavioral* and *cognitive* styles.

Model Structure

Table 4–4 presents our working model and lists the key words for each style. Reference to this table will be important to more fully understand and use the model.

Definitions for the eight emotional styles, eight physical styles, and eight cognitive styles are presented in Tables 4–1, 4–5, and 4–6. The physical styles are termed affiliative, outgoing, venturesome, restless, autonomous, introspective, regulated, and amicable. The styles for the cogni-

TABLE 4–4   Personal Styles Summary

EMOTIONAL STYLES	PHYSICAL STYLES	COGNITIVE STYLES
Zestful	Affiliative	Ideological
Expansive	Outgoing	Theoretical
Confrontive	Venturesome	Divergent
Restive	Restless	Individualistic
Reserved	Autonomous	Empirical
Modest	Introspective	Realistic
Patient	Regulated	Convergent
Empathic	Amicable	Conventional

Source: Adapted from J. T. Kunce, C. S. Cope, and R. M. Newton, *Manual for the Personal Styles Analysis* (Columbia, Mo.: Educational and Psychological Consultants, 1986).

TABLE 4–5   Physical Styles Definitions

Affiliative	Seeks approval and recognition through group activities, being a good team member, accepting what others deem important.
Outgoing	Seeks physical stimulations and thrills through exciting activities, participating in competitive games, or lively parties.
Venturesome	Seeks risky and daring challenges through adventurous activities, displaying an energetic, vigorous, and sometimes careless style.
Restless	Seeks varied and novel experiences through changeable activities, becoming bored with repetitive or confining tasks.
Autonomous	Seeks independent and self-directed activities through freelance activities, following one's inclinations.
Introspective	Seeks inner stimulation and gratification through self-imposed goals, showing a contemplative, sometimes preoccupied demeanor.
Regulated	Seeks safety and security through conservative activities, proceeding cautiously and carefully.
Amicable	Seeks harmony and consistency through peaceful activities, finding satisfaction in orderly and stable environments.

Source: J. T. Kunce, C. S. Cope, and R. M. Newton, *Manual for the Personal Styles Analysis* (Columbia, Mo.: Educational and Psychological Consultants, 1986).

TABLE 4–6   Cognitive Styles Definitions

Ideological	Views events from a set of beliefs from a social perspective, tending to draw conclusions from ideas rather than facts.
Theoretical	Views events from a philosophical perspective, tending to direct attention to political, theoretical, or religious ideas.
Divergent	Views events from a general, overall perspective, tending to engage in a variety of cultural, esthetic, or academic activities.
Individualistic	Views events from a personal perspective, tending to question existing premises and ideas.
Empirical	Views events from a cause-effect perspective, tending to require observable evidence to change existing beliefs.
Realistic	Views events from a commonsense perspective, tending to engage in goal-directed, problem-solving activities.
Convergent	Views events from a systematic perspective, tending to prefer exacting and detailed operations.
Conventional	Views events from a conforming and conservative perspective, tending to settle or avoid uncertainties as much as possible.

Source: J. T. Kunce, C. S. Cope, and R. M. Newton, *Manual for the Personal Styles Analysis* (Columbia, Mo.: Educational and Psychological Consultants, 1986).

tive mode are termed ideological, theoretical, divergent, individualistic, empirical, realistic, convergent, and conventional. Fig. 4–4 illustrates the circumplex relationship for the terms in each of the three modes. Note that these terms form sets of bipolar dimensions such as affiliative versus autonomous, venturesome versus regulated, and ideological versus empirical.

The personal styles model defines relatively discrete and interrelated aspects of a person's predispositions to behave in each of three modes—

Emotional Styles Circumplex

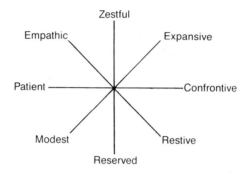

Physical Styles Circumplex

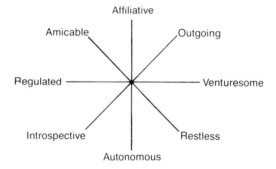

Cognitive Styles Circumplex

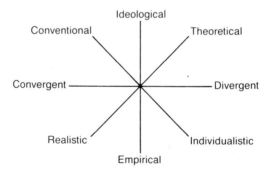

FIGURE 4–4   Emotional, physical, and cognitive styles circumplexes. (Adapted from J. T. Kunce, C. S. Cope, and R. M. Newton, *Manual for the Personal Styles Analysis* [Columbia, Mo.: Educational and Psychological Consultants, 1986].)

emotionally, physically, and cognitively. A firm conceptual grasp of Fig. 4–4 and the style definitions will be essential for their use in personal styles analysis.

Model Clarification

We have identified five aspects of the model that have particular meaning for interpreting personal styles. These aspects follow directly from the structure of the circumplex and the independence of each of the styles in one mode from those in the other two modes.

First, a person's most characteristic personal style disposition in any one mode (for example, zestful in the emotional mode) normally will be accompanied by strong dispositions on adjacent styles (for example, zestful with expansive and empathic) in that particular circumplex. In addition, the weakest dispositions can be expected to lie in the diagonally opposite sectors. For example, if modest, reserved, and restive have weak dispositions, then zestful, expansive, and empathic will have stronger dispositions.

Second, it is important to understand the significance of the model structure that makes each of the modes—emotional, physical, and cognitive—independent of each other. Note that any one style, such as zestful in the emotional mode, does not have to correspond to any one particular style in the other modes (Fig. 4–4). Predispositions in one circumplex may or may not correspond to a client's having predispositions in corresponding positions in the other circumplexes. Thus while one person's style could be characterized by zestful, affiliative, and ideological (the styles diagrammed at the top of each circumplex), the styles for another person could be mixed, such as zestful, autonomous, and empirical.

A third, and somewhat speculative, consideration is that when concurrence occurs in the relative positions of a person's predominant styles in each of the three circumplexes, a relatively clear-cut personality type is present. For example, Maccoby (1976) categorizes his therapy clients (who were mostly business executives) into four types: company man, gamesman, jungle hunter, and craftsman. One could hypothesize concurrence of circumplex position of personal styles across our three personal modes of emotional, physical, and cognitive (Fig. 4–4) as follows:

Company man	Empathic, amicable, conventional
Gamesman	Expansive, outgoing, theoretical
Jungle fighter	Restive, restless, individualistic
Craftsman	Modest, introspective, realistic

In a way, the correspondence between circumplex positions across the three modes could be viewed as analogous to notes on a musical scale being an octave apart. Striking the same note in three octaves increases the clarity and intensity of that note, but striking different notes adds to tonal complexity. Hence, the company man, gamesman, and so on, become clearly recognized types. In terms of the personality assessment formulations (Gittinger, 1964) these types might be described as showing uncompensated, natural behaviors. Personality types described by the PAS system as "compensated" might be analogous to the condition where the predominant styles in one mode do not share the same relative circumplex position as the predominant styles in the other modes.

A fourth and very crucial aspect of the model is that no one personal style should be considered as better or more adaptive than another. Some of the adjectives and terms we have used may have different social desirability appeal. Zestful in our society, for example, may be perceived in general as being more socially desirable than reserved. These styles, however, have equally adaptive or maladaptive consequences depending on the environmental circumstances and demands. Merrill and Reid (1981) found no difference in supervisory ratings of work performance of employees according to their categories of amiable, expressive, driver, and analytical.

Although no personal style is best, it is further assumed that each style, given an appropriate work and social environment, has unique, adaptive, and coping values. Concurrently, each style carries certain liabilities. Kunce and Anderson (1976) postulate positive and counterpart negative descriptors for elevated series on each MMPI scale. In like fashion, it would be possible to specify characteristics for any one style that might pose adaptive difficulties in stressful situations. For example, extremely zestful behavior may be perceived as being pollyannaish by others; extremely restive behavior may be perceived as being irritable.

A final and crucial consideration is that determination of a person's style as more like one side of a continuum than the other (for example, zestful-reserved) does not mean that he or she does not possess the "opposite" characteristic. A zestful person can display reserved behavior, and a reserved person zestful behavior. The *probabilities* of exhibiting one style or the other is the aspect that is different. This situation is directly comparable to being characterized as righthanded or lefthanded. Both hands can be used in concert as well as independently, even though certain preferences clearly exist for most people. The conceptualization of personality style according to the Myers-Briggs type indicator is also directly comparable to our position.

Face Validity

Definitions for the personal styles model have been formulated as much as possible in clear and meaningful ways so that they are readily understandable to the client in terms of everyday life. Furthermore, it would be possible to use these definitions to categorize specific occupations into requisite personal styles according to our circumplex model, as Holland (1985) has typed occupations according to his hexagonal model. For the purposes of this chapter, we believe it will be more productive to use our model to develop a better understanding of a client's personal styles as they relate to work/social demands than to specific occupational choice. Discussion with the client of his or her personal style predispositions and an analysis of their role in career adjustment will have face validity in terms of their fit with objectively observable events.

PERSONAL STYLES ASSESSMENT

The assessment of personal styles can be done quickly and in a straightforward manner. All that is required is a determination of client need for personal styles analysis, the eight definitions for each style in three modes, a scoring sheet, and some simple calculations for "smoothing" the curve. The basic data collected can be client self-ratings, ratings made by family members or friends, or any combination thereof.

Determining the Need

The first step is to determine whether personal styles analysis will be useful for a client. A pivotal factor is the degree to which a client shows concern around problems associated with the satisfaction and satisfactoriness of current or anticipated role and functions. The conflicts may be either interpersonal, such as conflicts between personal styles of the client and those of peers or supervisors, or occupational such as between personal styles and career demands. If these problems appear to be related directly to the client's own pattern of personal styles, the use of a personal styles analysis could be explored. If it turns out that specific occupational information, educational/career opportunities, or psychological disturbance is more clearly the major concern, other procedures and techniques may be more appropriate.

Collecting the Data

Assuming that a person shows concern that his or her unique personal styles may be a factor in work or social satisfactions, the counselor might explain the objective of a personal styles analysis. An adaptation of the following introductory statements could be used:

> A person's pattern of personal predisposition, or styles, is strongly interrelated with one's work and social satisfactions. Each person's unique pattern of styles presents strengths and liabilities in respect to what one's environment demands. An extrovert may be frustrated with an introvert who keeps thoughts and feelings private; an introvert may be frustrated with an extrovert who might talk too much; an imaginative person may be bored with details; a practical person irritated by grandiose schemes; and so on. It is

possible for us to examine and evaluate your special ways of behaving that could be important to your understanding of how you fit into the world around you. For example, do you view a person who is different from you as having more desirable or less desirable personal characteristics? When can such differences be complementary or antagonistic?

The first step in our analysis is to find out how you respond to twenty-four questions that provide key information about your basic personal styles. Would you be interested in finding out more about yourself? (Adapted from Kunce, Cope, and Newton, 1986)

The next step, given client readiness, is for the counselor to read aloud to the client each of the personal styles statements and to record the client's responses to each. The statements in Tables 4–1, 4–5, and 4–6 should be used and items read in that sequence. In some instances it may also be desirable to give the client a copy of these statements to read along with you.

After each statement is read, ask the client to indicate the degree of accuracy to which the description fits his or her personal style. The client can be asked simply to respond true or false. We recommend, however, a ten-point scale where 1 signifies "Not at all like me" and 10 signifies "Very much like me." To facilitate client responding, present a card showing the following descriptors:

1	2	3	4	5	6	7	8	9	10
Not at all like me	Does not fit me well	A little more unlike me than like me			A little more like me than unlike me		Fits pretty well		Very much like me

Be certain that the client understands the statements. Avoid as much as possible defining terms or providing your own interpretation of the statements (which invariably fosters experimenter bias). When a client puzzles over a response as "parts of it are like me and parts not," encourage a 5 or 6 rating to indicate a best guess. Encourage the client to respond quickly to the gist of each statement and not to dwell on any one adjective or phrase.

Recording and Quantifying Data

The form presented in Fig. 4–5 can be used to record client ratings and to compute personal style scores. Record the client's rating for each of the eight statements for each of the three modes in the appropriate blanks. Personal style total scores are obtained for each style by "curve smoothing." For example, under the emotional mode the total score for zestful equals the zestful rating (1) plus the ratings for expansive (2) and for empathic (8).

The total score for expansive is the ratings for (2) plus (3) plus (1). Similarly, the score for any one rating equals the rating for that statement plus the ratings for the two adjacent statements according to their position in the circumplex. The total scores for each style can be plotted according to the circumplex model in Fig. 4–5 and used in carrying out a personal styles analysis. Note that the "response set" that a client may employ (tending to choose moderate or extreme ratings) will not detract from style identification. Given the bipolar nature of the styles identified for each circumplex, it is the difference between opposite styles that determines the relative strength of a predisposition, not the magnitude of any one score. It is possible to infer the relative strengths of the predispositions by finding the highest score across the three circumplexes and by considering the other scores in relationship to it.

PERSONAL STYLES ANALYSIS AND CAREER ASSESSMENT AND COUNSELING

In this section we discuss how information from the personal styles analysis can be used with your clients either in career planning and decision making or in dealing with other events and relationships in their lives. Helping them gain knowledge of their preferred ways of behaving, that is, their own unique life-styles, should increase self-understanding. This self-understanding can add to a client's ability to deal more effectively with various situations: career decisions, relationships in the workplace, and other personal relationships and events. The focus in this book has been on life-span career planning and on a broad, total life definition of career. Use of life-style information in career assessment and counseling is consistent with and can contribute to this encompassing concept of life career development.

Personal Styles Analysis and Careers

Life-style information in some form has been used in career assessment and counseling for a long time. The Myers-Briggs type indicator, based on Jungian theory of psychological types, is one instrument that has been used in this capacity. Myers (1980) discusses the relevance of life-style information in the career counseling process. In a comparable manner Merrill and Reid (1981) discuss their research and the use of their four life-styles in the business world.

The research of both Myers (1975) and Merrill and Reid (1981) indicates that information about basic life-styles may be more helpful in considering the roles and functions that one may prefer in an occupation than in

Emotional Style Ratings:

(1)__ + (2)__ + (8)__ = ___
(2)__ + (3)__ + (1)__ = ___
(3)__ + (4)__ + (2)__ = ___
(4)__ + (5)__ + (3)__ = ___
(5)__ + (6)__ + (4)__ = ___
(6)__ + (7)__ + (5)__ = ___
(7)__ + (8)__ + (6)__ = ___
(8)__ + (1)__ + (7)__ = ___

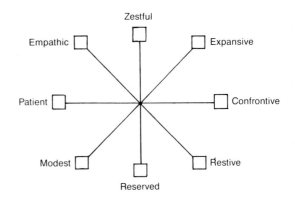

Physical Style Ratings:

(1)__ + (2)__ + (8)__ = ___
(2)__ + (3)__ + (1)__ = ___
(3)__ + (4)__ + (2)__ = ___
(4)__ + (5)__ + (3)__ = ___
(5)__ + (6)__ + (4)__ = ___
(6)__ + (7)__ + (5)__ = ___
(7)__ + (8)__ + (6)__ = ___
(8)__ + (1)__ + (7)__ = ___

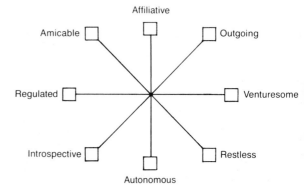

Cognitive Style Ratings:

(1)__ + (2)__ + (8)__ = ___
(2)__ + (3)__ + (1)__ = ___
(3)__ + (4)__ + (2)__ = ___
(4)__ + (5)__ + (3)__ = ___
(5)__ + (6)__ + (4)__ = ___
(6)__ + (7)__ + (5)__ = ___
(7)__ + (8)__ + (6)__ = ___
(8)__ + (1)__ + (7)__ = ___

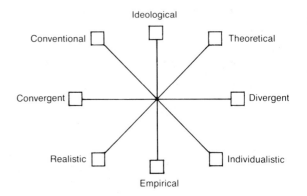

FIGURE 4-5   Personal styles summary sheet. (Adapted from J. T. Kunce, C. S. Cope, and R. M. Newton, *Manual for the Personal Styles Analysis* [Columbia, Mo.: Educational and Psychological Consultants, 1986].)

helping decide on a specific occupation. These authors believe that any of their basic life-styles may be found in any occupation and that each style can be adaptive in any occupation. They found no correlation between style and success. Thus a life-style that an individual has developed does not automatically prevent going into any occupation of one's choice. No occupation or job is eliminated as a possibility for any one person on the basis of life-style. It would appear that successful people have learned how to use their own particular styles in an adaptive way in their particular situation.

Life-style information is most useful in suggesting specific roles and/or functions that a person may prefer in work and social situations. Choice of a specific occupation, for example, may not depend on a specific life-style, although what a client prefers doing or gains satisfaction from may be greatly influenced by life-style (McCaulley, 1981; Merrill and Reid, 1981). Thus information about life-style would seem more helpful in long-term career planning than in making a specific decision such as what academic courses to enroll in next semester.

An example of how personality styles analysis may relate to career preferences can be illustrated using the occupation of rehabilitation counselor. Kunce and Derrieux (1984) delineate from available research two types of rehabilitation counselors according to their primary roles and functions in the rehabilitation agency: the case manager and the therapist. The case manager is described as goal-directed with a high energy level and with excellent time-management skills. These counselors prefer working with less difficult clients, have a high rate of community involvement, achieve a high rate of successful case closures, and spend the least amount of money on rehabilitation services. The therapist deals with more difficult cases, spends more money and time per client, has fewer successful closures per year, and carries smaller caseloads.

The personality styles profiles that we believe are most compatible with the roles and functions expected of these two counselors are presented in Table 4–7. In the emotional mode the typical therapist might score highest in the patient and empathic styles; the case manager, in the zestful, expansive, and confrontive styles. The physical mode would probably show sharper differences between counselor styles, with the two counselors scoring on opposite sides of the circumplex. Descriptors hypothesized for the therapist are introspective, regulated, and amicable; for the case manager, outgoing, and venturesome. In the cognitive mode the therapist might score highest in the theoretical, divergent, and individualistic styles, and the case manager in the realistic, convergent, and conventional styles. Fig. 4–6 illustrates the different personal styles that may be most compatible with job satisfaction and performance according to job role and function.

The therapist's preferred styles can be described, according to our

TABLE 4–7   Personality Styles Differences between Rehabilitation Counselor Therapist and Case Manager Types

BEHAVIORAL MODE	COUNSELOR TYPE	PERSONAL STYLE
Emotional mode	Therapist	Empathic and patient
	Case manager	Zestful, expansive, confrontive
Physical mode	Therapist	Introspective, regulated, amicable
	Case manager	Outgoing and venturesome
Cognitive mode	Therapist	Theoretical, divergent, individualistic
	Case manager	Conventional, convergent, realistic

specific style definitions, as considerate, calm, and responding in concert with emotions of others; taking time to carefully evaluate the nature of a client's problem; and thinking of alternate ways that the client could cope. The preferred life-styles of a case manager would likely be enthusiastic, energetic, and straightforward; venturesome and actively seeking variety; and able to make decisions quickly and willing to take responsibility for those decisions. Differences in styles are relative, not absolute. As stated earlier, everyone has behaviors inherent in all styles and does at times use behaviors other than the dominant predispositions. The therapist obviously must be able to be confrontive as well as patient in relating to a client. The case manager who must often be confrontive in the role of client advocate also must be able to show patience.

Both types of rehabilitation counselors can be equally successful. Difficulties may arise, however, when a counselor with personal style predispositions corresponding to therapist is expected to perform as a case manager and vice versa. Such counselors may be dissatisfied with roles and functions, and their agencies with counselor behavior. Obtaining information about one's preferred life-style in a situation such as this can be helpful in career planning, job seeking, and job adjustment.

An example of personal style differences of two psychologists, A and B, is shown in Figs. 4–7 and 4–8. These two profiles also will be used to demonstrate, step by step, the procedures used in a personal styles assessment. Ratings were obtained from these two persons using the ten-point Likert-type scale described earlier. The ratings for each style definition under the three modes were recorded next to the numbers in the extreme left-hand column on the personal styles summary sheet. The first number in the emotional mode is for the zestful rating, the second number for the expansive rating, the third for confrontive, and so on, proceeding clockwise around the circumplex. Note that the first number in the left-hand column for each mode is always for the style at the top of the circumplex.

Emotional Styles Circumplex

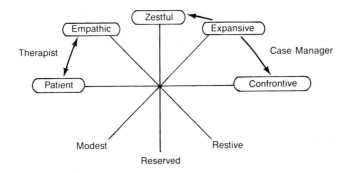

Physical Styles Circumplex

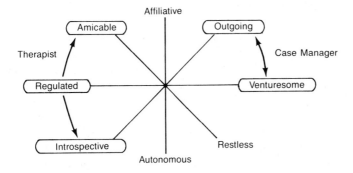

Cognitive Styles Circumplex

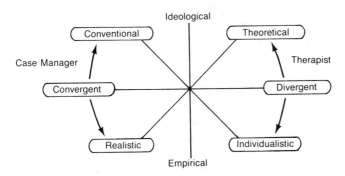

FIGURE 4–6   Rehabilitation counselor therapist and case manager predominant styles.

After recording in column 1 the ratings for all twenty-four definitions, the second step is curve smoothing. This is accomplished for the emotional mode as follows: the ratings in column 2 are the same ratings recorded in column 1 except that one starts with the second rating in the circumplex and proceeds in clockwise fashion around the circumplex. Thus the first blank in column 2 is for the expansive rating, the second blank for confrontive, and so on. Similarly, the blanks in column 3 are once again for the same set of emotional ratings, but the first blank in this column is for the eighth rating, empathic, the second for the zestful, the third for confrontive. Note that these numbers can be copied from the original ratings in column 1. The curve smoothing is accomplished by adding the three scores in one row. In Fig. 4–7 the smoothed score for *zestful* equals the ratings for zestful plus expansive plus empathic, which is 9 + 7 + 8, or 24. The score for *expansive* equals the ratings for expansive plus confrontive plus zestful, which is 7 + 3 + 9, or 19. This procedure is followed for all twenty-four ratings. The total smoothed score for each style is entered into the corresponding box in the appropriate circumplex. In Fig. 4–7 the number 24 is recorded in the box for the zestful style, 19 in the expansive box, and so on.

The third step is to select and circle the four highest scores for each of the three modes. In Fig. 4–7 the highest scores in the emotional mode are zestful (24) and empathic (24). The other two highest scores for this mode are 19 for expansive and 18 for patient. The fourth step is checking the differences between these four high scores and their corresponding opposite scores. The opposite of zestful is reserved, and for this person the two scores are 24 and 9, respectively. The opposite of empathic is restive and the scores are also 24 and 9, respectively. For both of these zestful-reserved and empathic-restive dimensions, the difference between the bipolar scores is 15. Expansive, the third highest score, is 7 points higher than its opposite, modest. The fourth highest score, patient, is only 4 points higher than its opposite, confrontive. In this profile the two styles rating highest in the emotional mode, therefore, have the greatest differences between them and their opposites. These highest styles, zestful and empathic, are starred as being the strongest preferred styles for that mode. The same procedure should be used to analyze the scores from the physical and cognitive circumplexes.

Finally, refer to the personal styles definitions (Tables 4–1, 4–5, and 4–6) to obtain a description of preferred styles for psychologist A. These statements can be used to interpret preferred styles for the person being assessed. This information should always be given as tentative and as suggestive of preferences, not as fact. Ask the client how the ideas from the life-style profile "fits." Does the client view his or her behavior as like this or different? If different, what are the differences? Information on life-style presented in this way can be used effectively for discussion and exploration

Emotional Mode Ratings:

(1) 9 + (2) 7 + (8) 8 = 24
(2) 7 + (3) 3 + (1) 9 = 19
(3) 3 + (4) 4 + (2) 7 = 14
(4) 4 + (5) 2 + (3) 3 = 9
(5) 2 + (6) 3 + (4) 4 = 9
(6) 3 + (7) 7 + (5) 2 = 12
(7) 7 + (8) 8 + (6) 3 = 18
(8) 8 + (1) 9 + (7) 7 = 24

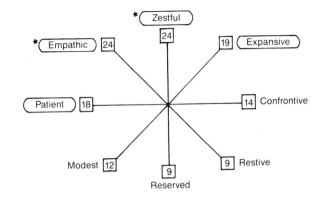

Physical Style Ratings:

(1) 6 + (2) 4 + (8) 6 = 16
(2) 4 + (3) 2 + (1) 6 = 12
(3) 2 + (4) 6 + (2) 4 = 12
(4) 6 + (5) 9 + (3) 2 = 17
(5) 9 + (6) 8 + (4) 6 = 23
(6) 8 + (7) 6 + (5) 9 = 23
(7) 6 + (8) 6 + (6) 8 = 20
(8) 6 + (1) 6 + (7) 6 = 18

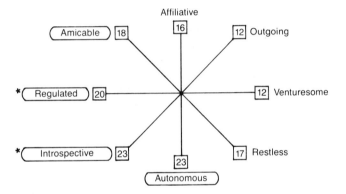

Cognitive Style Ratings:

(1) 3 + (2) 6 + (8) 2 = 11
(2) 6 + (3) 7 + (1) 3 = 16
(3) 7 + (4) 8 + (2) 6 = 21
(4) 8 + (5) 8 + (3) 7 = 23
(5) 8 + (6) 6 + (4) 8 = 22
(6) 6 + (7) 4 + (5) 8 = 18
(7) 4 + (8) 2 + (6) 6 = 12
(8) 2 + (1) 3 + (7) 4 = 9

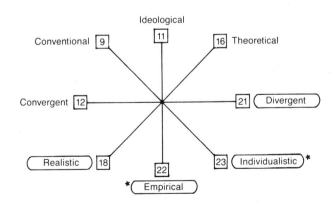

FIGURE 4–7 Personal styles summary sheet: Psychologist A.

Emotional Mode Ratings:

(1) 4 + (2) 3 + (8) 6 = 13
(2) 3 + (3) 2 + (1) 4 = 9
(3) 2 + (4) 4 + (2) 3 = 9
(4) 4 + (5) 8 + (3) 2 = 14
(5) 8 + (6) 8 + (4) 4 = 20
(6) 8 + (7) 8 + (5) 8 = 24
(7) 8 + (8) 6 + (6) 8 = 22
(8) 6 + (1) 4 + (7) 8 = 18

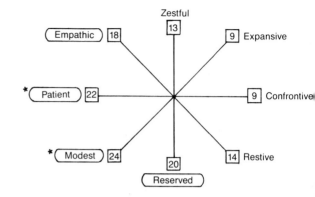

Physical Style Ratings:

(1) 4 + (2) 3 + (8) 6 = 13
(2) 3 + (3) 4 + (1) 4 = 11
(3) 4 + (4) 8 + (2) 3 = 15
(4) 8 + (5) 9 + (3) 4 = 21
(5) 9 + (6) 6 + (4) 8 = 23
(6) 6 + (7) 5 + (5) 9 = 20
(7) 5 + (8) 6 + (6) 6 = 17
(8) 6 + (1) 4 + (7) 5 = 15

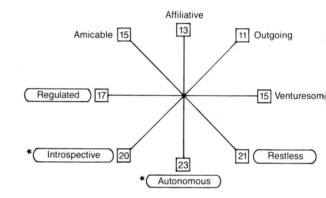

Cognitive Style Ratings:

(1) 6 + (2) 5 + (8) 4 = 15
(2) 5 + (3) 7 + (1) 6 = 18
(3) 7 + (4) 9 + (2) 5 = 21
(4) 9 + (5) 8 + (3) 7 = 24
(5) 8 + (6) 7 + (4) 9 = 24
(6) 7 + (7) 3 + (5) 8 = 18
(7) 3 + (8) 4 + (6) 7 = 14
(8) 4 + (1) 6 + (7) 3 = 13

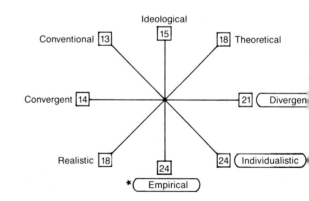

FIGURE 4–8 Personal styles summary sheet: Psychologist B.

in career assessment and counseling. How the client views this information is important for helping him or her explore occupations, specialty areas within occupations, and in various career decisions and overall planning.

In our example the statements from the emotional style definitions (Table 4–1) can be used to indicate that psychologist A's primary predispositions for zestful are "shows an enthusiastic and optimistic disposition, emphasizing the positive rather than negative aspects of events"; and for empathic, "shows a sympathetic and understanding disposition, responding in concert with emotions of others." Similarly, behavioral definitions for the styles of patient and modest for psychologist B can be formulated. By comparing the profiles in Figs. 4–7 and 4–8, it is evident that differences exist between psychologists A and B in the emotional mode, while their styles in the physical and cognitive modes are quite similar. Statements for the similarities and differences for all of their preferred styles can be obtained by referring to the definitions in Tables 4–1, 4–5, and 4–6.

Considering these two profiles, the assumption could be made that both of these individuals would prefer work situations that provide autonomy, independence, and the freedom to investigate and analyze problems. The greatest difference may be that psychologist A would seek out and prefer situations that provide a great deal of emotional interaction with others, while psychologist B may prefer and be more comfortable in carrying out work in a more private fashion. Although both of these psychologists have enjoyed and have been effective in teaching, service, and research activities, the expressed occupational preferences for these two individuals have been teaching for A and research for B.

Differences and similarities in personal styles, such as we have explored for rehabilitation counselors and psychologists, can be projected into almost any occupational field, such as law, medicine, science, business, teaching, engineering, accounting, and construction. Consider the probable differences in life-style for a trial lawyer versus a lawyer who prefers to settle estates. The trial lawyer will need more of an expansive and confrontive emotional style. Consider also that the preferred life-styles may vary for physicians according to their careers as a general practitioner, researcher, teacher, and hospital administrator.

The impact of life-style on careers has research as well as empirical support. Myers and Davis (1964) studied more than 5000 medical students in the early 1950s using the Myers-Briggs type indicator. They found significant differences in life-style types for those who chose surgery versus psychiatry. In a follow-up study twelve years later they found that the subsequent medical specialties were significantly associated with the directions predicted by life-style types. We would therefore urge counselors to consider life-style along with other critical factors such as education, job opportunities, and mobility in career counseling.

Interpersonal Analysis of Life-Styles

Life-style information can be used in exploring interpersonal interactions in the work and social environments, including co-workers, supervisors, administrators, consumers, friends, and spouses. Consider, for example, the two rehabilitation counselors discussed earlier, the therapist and the case manager. These two counselors may complement each other in an agency that emphasizes both types of services. However, in an agency where the focus is on one type of service in preference to another, conflicts may arise for the person "out of step." Also, if one of these counselors becomes the supervisor of the other, the two may or may not work well together. If problems arise, exploration of preferred life-styles would be in order. Understanding that there are style differences may be all that is needed to improve a situation. Of greater benefit would be exploration of how people with different preferred styles can complement each other, how the strengths of each can help an organization and those with whom one works. Merrill and Reid (1981) discuss these ideas in detail.

Referring again to the two rehabilitation counselors, conflicts may arise between consumers of the agency's services (the client) and the counselor. If the client prefers "therapist" counseling and the counselor is a "case manager," conflicts may arise over services with neither understanding what is wrong.

Information about life-styles can also be used in counseling about interpersonal interactions as in friendship problems, roommate problems, and marital problems. Schroeder (1979) found that difficulties between roommates were reduced when personality types were taken into account in roommate matching. A special contribution of a personal styles concept in career counseling is its potential for helping clients understand more fully how their preferred styles influence their actions and reactions to others around them in social as well as work environments. Given a better understanding, clients become better prepared to accept differences in styles from a nonjudgmental stance, to adapt to another's style, and to modify their own style where accommodations are desired or required.

ADDITIONAL CONSIDERATIONS AND COMMENTS

In this final section we discuss a number of points and issues that are important for understanding and applying our model for personal styles analysis. Included are a list of specific assessment considerations of response style ratings, a discussion of personal style adaptive and maladaptive behavioral implications, and some comparisons of Holland's hexagon model and the Myers-Briggs types with our model.

Response Style Ratings

A person's responses to the twenty-four personal style statements have a number of behavioral and assessment validity implications. The following list summarizes some of the issues that could be important to explore with a client.

1. *Client-Observer Congruence.* Are the client's self-ratings similar to those that a counselor, friend, or spouse might use in describing the client? What are the interpersonal and intrapersonal implications of existent discrepancies?

2. *Interpersonal Interactions.* What are the effects of similarities and differences between the client's personal styles and the styles of significant others, such as therapist, spouse, boss, and friend?

3. *Personal Style Acceptance.* Is the client accepting of his or her own personal styles, or does he or she perceive other styles as more desirable?

4. *Personal Style Stability.* Does the client see a developmental change in his or her styles from the past and into the future? How might such change relate to careers?

5. *Complementary Styles.* Does the personal styles analysis show high ratings for opposite sides of a continuum, such as on regulated and venturesome? Does the "contradiction" imply complementary behavior accommodations or intrapsychic conflict?

6. *Style Rigidity.* Does the analysis show that a client has made exceptionally low ratings on one side of a continuum and exceptionally high ratings on another? Could this represent either satisfaction with the primary disposition or discomfort with using alternate behavioral styles?

7. *Balanced Style.* Do client responses show few clearly defined personal predispositions? Does this increase a client's behavioral flexibility or reflect client indecisiveness?

8. *Mode Exaggeration.* Does the client show evidence of rating items in one mode consistently higher (or lower) than styles in the other modes? Would, for example, very high ratings in the cognitive mode indicate an overly intellectualizing style?

9. *Mode Congruence.* Does a client endorse styles that occupy the same related circumplex position regardless of mode? Does this pattern influence stereotypical perception of the client?

10. *Response Validity.* Does the client respond to all personal style statements with extreme ratings at only one end or at both ends of the ten-point continuum? Such patterns may have either personal style or test validity implications.

We have not presented answers to these questions. Our intention is simply to provide the counselor with key items to stimulate exploration and discussion of response styles implications with a client.

Personal Adjustment Implications

We have deliberately focused on the positive aspects of personal adjustment in our life-styles analysis. The psychological literature is redundant with a persistent interpretation of personality from a psychopatholo-gical perspective (for example, Millon, 1984). Leary (1957), Kunce (1979), and Kunce and Anderson (1976, 1984) have argued that equal attention should be given to adaptive behaviors and that these adaptive behaviors, under stress, have maladaptive counterparts. Leary hypothesizes that a person's adaptive predisposition, such as managerial, will change to malad-aptive autocratic behavior under increasing stress. The predisposition to "manage, direct, and lead" will change to "provokes obedience" and "domi-nate, boss, and order." We are undertaking research to verify maladaptive characteristics for each of our twenty-four styles but believe it would be counterproductive to introduce them here. It is much more important from a career perspective to consider the kinds of favorable or unfavorable consequences that each of our twenty-four styles might have in terms of environmental demands; that is, how do roles, functions, and expectations interact with a person's basic styles?

Model Comparison

Our personal styles model differs from Holland's hexagonal model and the Myers-Briggs type indicator, which presently are widely used in career assessment and counseling (Holland, 1985; Pinkney, 1983). The research literature is replete with studies supporting the hexagonal rela-tionship of realistic, investigative, artistic, social, enterprising, and conven-tional. A few studies, however, suggest that the circular type arrangement of the six types may be oversimplified (Gati, 1979, 1982). In essence, the critical concerns are statistically based. First, data fail to show significant negative correlations between opposite types (for example, realistic with social) even though clearly significant correlations exist between adjacent pairs (for example, realistic with investigative and conventional). More im-portant, hierarchical analysis suggests that the six styles represent three modes with enterprising and conventional relating to a people/service mode, artistic and social to a self-expression mode, and realistic and investi-gative to a cognitive mode. The advantages of separating out three modes, as we have done, creates more flexibility than is currently possible using Holland's hexagonal model.

In our opinion the Myers-Briggs formulations permit greater flexibil-ity in describing personality styles than does the Holland hexagonal model. Our basic criticism of the Myers-Briggs model is in what we believe to be inadequate differentiation between styles and modes. For example, their conceptualization places thinking and feeling types at opposite ends of a continuum. Thus a person cannot be a thinking type and a feeling type simultaneously. In contrast, research evidence supports the contention that they are independent modalities (Kunce and Tamkin, 1981; Skinner and Jackson, 1978). Our model permits specific delineation of a person's feelings and cognitions, for example, a person can be empathic and either theoretical or realistic.

Both the Holland and the Myers-Briggs models are widely accepted as useful counseling tools. They have a wide base of empirical and research support. The particular advantage of our procedure is to offer greater precision of behavioral description of life-styles and to present a procedure that can obtain data in a relatively simple and straightforward manner. The usefulness of the data at the present time, however, will depend heavily on the counselor's own expertise in being able to adequately address the life-style expectations of various career roles and functions in discussion with the client. To help develop this expertise, we urge counselors to first try out life-style analysis on themselves and willing associates.

We have presented a model for personal styles analysis that provides a holistic appraisal of a person's behavioral predispositions in each of three behavioral domains: emotional, physical, and cognitive. The model provides for a comprehensive yet highly individualistic description of a person's personal styles with 2^{12}, or 4096, unique combinations of descriptive terms possible. Other behavioral domains, such as time orientation and ethical values, conceivably could be constructed in circumplex fashion to add further complexity to this model. We believe for practical purposes that the total number of behavioral domains should be few in order to facilitate discussion with the client. In conclusion, our procedure of personal styles analysis, used in conjunction with other career counseling techniques, can efficiently assist clients understand themselves more fully with respect to career roles, functions, and expectations across the life span.

REFERENCES

ADLER, A., "Degree of Activity," in *The Individual Psychology of Alfred Adler: A Systematic Presentation in Selections from his Writings*, eds. H. L. Ansbacher and R. R. Ansbacher. New York: Basic Books, 1956.

GATI, I., "A Hierarchial Model for the Structure of Vocational Interest," *Journal of Vocational Behavior*, 15 (1979), 90–106.

———, "Testing Models for the Structure of Vocational Interests," *Journal of Vocational Behavior*, 21 (1982), 164–82.

GITTINGER, J., *Personality Assessment System.* New York: Human Ecology Fund, 1964.

HOLLAND, J., *Making Vocational Choices: A Theory of Vocational Personalities and Work Environments.* Englewood Cliffs, N.J.: Prentice-Hall, 1985.

JUNG, C. G., *Psychological Types.* London: Rutledge & Kegan Paul, 1923.

KEIRSEY, D., and BATES, M., *Please Understand Me: An Essay on Temperamental Styles*, DelMar, Calif.: Prometheus Nemesis Books, 1978.

KIRBY, P., *Cognitive Style, Learning Style, and Transfer Skill Acquisition.* Columbus, Ohio: National Center for Research in Vocational Education, 1979.

KRAUSKOPF, C., and DAVIS, K., *Studies of the Normal Personality.* Columbia, Mo.: University of Missouri–Columbia Testing and Counseling Service, 1969.

KRUG, S., *The Adult Personality Inventory.* Champaign, Ill.: Institute for Personality and Ability Testing, 1984.

KUNCE, J. T., "MMPI Scores and Adaptive Behavior," in *MMPI Clinical and Research Trends,* ed. C. Newmark. New York: Praeger, 1979.

————, and ANDERSON, W., "Normalizing the MMPI," *Journal of Clinical Psychology,* 32 (1976), 776–80.

————, and ————, "Perspectives on Uses of the MMPI in Nonpsychiatric Settings," in *Advances in Psychological Assessment,* vol. 6. eds. P. McReynolds and G. Chelune. San Francisco: Jossey-Bass, 1984.

————, COPE, C. S., and NEWTON, R. M., *Manual for the Personal Styles Analysis.* Columbia, Mo.: Educational and Psychological Consultants, 1986.

————, and DERRIEUX, G. A., "Evaluating Rehabilitation Counselor Effectiveness," in *Critical Issues in Rehabilitation Counseling,* eds. W. G. Emener, A. Patrick, and D. K. Hollingsworth. Springfield, Ill.: Charles C Thomas, 1984.

————, and TAMKIN, A., "Rorschach Movement and Color Responses and MMPI Social Extraversion and Thinking Introversion Personality Types," *Journal of Personality Assessment,* 45 (1981), 5–10.

LEARY, T., *Interpersonal Diagnosis of Personality: A Function Theory and Methodology for Personality Evaluation.* New York: Ronald Press, 1957.

MACCOBY, M., *The Gamesman: The New Corporate Leaders.* New York: Simon & Schuster, 1976.

MCCAULLEY, M. H., *The Myers Longitudinal Medical Study.* Gainesville, Fla.: Center for Applications of Psychological Type, 1977.

————, "Jung's Theory of Psychological Types and the Myers-Briggs Type Indicator," in *Advances in Psychological Assessment,* vol. 5, ed. P. McReynolds. San Francisco: Jossey-Bass, 1981.

MERRILL, D. W., and REID, R. H., *Personal Styles and Effective Performance.* Radnor, Pa.: Chelton Book Co., 1981.

MILLON, T., "On the Renaissance of Personality Assessment and Personality Theory," *Journal of Personality Assessment,* 48 (1984), 450–66.

MYERS, I. B., *Manual: The Myers-Briggs Type Indicator.* Palo Alto, Calif.: Consulting Psychologists Press, 1975.

————, *Introduction to Type* (3rd ed.). Gainesville, Fla.: Center for Applications of Psychological Type, 1980.

————, and DAVIS, J. A., "Relations of Medical Students' Psychological Type to Their Specialties Twelve Years Later." Paper presented at the meeting of the American Psychological Association, Los Angeles, 1964.

O'DELL, J., "W. T. Barnum Explores the Computer," *Journal of Consulting and Clinical Psychology,* 28 (1972), 270–73.

PINKNEY, J., "The Myers-Briggs Type Indicator as an Alternative in Career Counseling," *Personnel and Guidance Journal,* 61 (1983), 173–77.

SCHROEDER, C. S., "Designing Ideal Staff Environments Through Milieu Management," *Journal of College Student Personnel,* 19 (1979), 129–35.

SKINNER, H., and JACKSON, D., "A Model of Psychopathology Based on an Integration of MMPI Actuarial Systems," *Journal of Consulting and Clinical Psychology,* 46 (1978), 231–38.

SNYDER, C., SHENKEL, R., and LOWREY, C., "Acceptance of Personality Interpretations: The 'Barnum Effect' and Beyond," *Journal of Consulting and Clinical Psychology,* 45 (1977), 104–14.

SPIELBARGER, C., GORSUCH, R., and LUSHENE, R., *STAI Manual.* Palo Alto, Calif.: Consulting Psychologists Press, 1970.

WATKINS, C. E., "The Individual Psychology of Alfred Adler: Toward an Adlerian Vocational Theory," *Journal of Vocational Behavior,* 24 (1984), 28–47.

WOOLLAMS, S., and BROWN, M., *TA: The Total Handbook of Transactional Analysis,* Englewood Cliffs, N.J.: Prentice-Hall, 1979.

Occupational
Card Sorts

The strong tendency in counseling to dichotomize self-exploration and occupational exploration as independent processes—that is, first to build up a picture of the client and only then to turn consideration of occupational information to "find" a "match"— must be overcome. "Bridges" between individual counselee and vocational life, if they are to be psychologically meaningful, must rest on dynamic as well as factual grounds. They must be largely self-created, not simply "found" in predetermined, generalized classification systems. They must be "personalized" or "custom-tailored," rather than "ready-made." (Prichard, 1962, p. 677)

Various techniques are available to help you better understand your clients, and, in turn, help your clients better understand themselves. Standardized and criterion-referenced tests and inventories provide comparisons of the client against a standard or with others as to interests, values, abilities, achievements, attitudes, and personality. Words such as *persuasive, abstract, outdoor,* and *mechanical* are used in these tests and inventories to describe client attributes.

You may also want to consider a technique that starts with and highlights the life career themes of your clients. To do this you will need a way to help your clients think about and express their themes or their ways of thinking about themselves, others, and the world in which they live. However, it does little good to ask, "What are your life career themes?" What is needed are techniques that present common, everyday stimuli from which clients' themes can be ascertained (Edmonds, 1979).

In Chapter 3 we described the use of a technique called life career assessment to accomplish this. In this chapter we present the occupational card sort, which uses occupational titles to elicit life career themes. Occupational titles are common, everyday terms, and even though a person may have stereotypical ideas about occupations, information can be obtained about how the person looks at himself or herself, at others, and the world in which he or she lives. Occupational titles are stimuli from which we can evoke a word picture of a person's themes.

Chapter 5 presents a discussion of some of the benefits of using occupational card sorts and describes ways to develop one. The Missouri Occupational Preference Inventory (MOPI) (Moore and Gysbers, 1980) is used to illustrate the use of an occupational card sort with clients. The chapter closes with some concluding thoughts about the use of occupational card sorts.

BENEFITS OF THE OCCUPATIONAL CARD SORT

The occupational card sort originally was suggested by Tyler (1961) in her address to the American Psychological Association's Division of Counseling Psychology. Since then it has been used and researched by a number of investigators including Dolliver (1964, 1982), Dolliver and Will (1977), and Jones (1979, 1980, 1983). The use of a card sort may:

- Promote career exploration (Cooper, 1976)
- Involve the individual to a greater degree (Dewey, 1974)
- Stimulate discussion about the reasons for certain choices (Dolliver, 1967)
- Reinforce natural curiosity about occupations
- Help individuals feel more relaxed because of the activity involved with sorting the cards
- Provide immediate feedback (Jones, 1980)
- Provide a nonthreatening activity (Jones, 1980)
- Facilitate an individual's career decision (Jones, 1979)

Often young people are searching for ways to increase their self-understanding and for help in career planning and career decision making. Adults may be concerned about low pay and the fringe benefits in their present work, stressful working conditions, a lack of interest in their present job, or the lack of challenge at work. Young people and adults with these and similar concerns will find that using an occupational card sort may assist them to understand their motives and values (themes), explore career options, understand the reasons behind their possible choices, and identify the next steps to guide further exploration.

DEVELOPING AN OCCUPATIONAL CARD SORT

There are a number of published occupational card sorts available. Not mentioned in Dolliver's 1982 review is a series of card sorts available from Career Research and Testing, San Jose, California (Knowdell, 1982), including ones on occupational interest, retirement activities, career values, and motivated skills. You can also develop your own card sort using whatever topics or issues you may wish. Occupational titles represent only one topic.

If you are planning to develop your own occupational card sort, there are a number of points to keep in mind. The first point to consider is the number of occupations (cards) to include in the sort. We recommend that during the actual sorting process with a client you use only fifty to sixty cards. You may wish to have more occupations (120 to 180) in your deck to draw from, however. A second point to consider is the mix of occupations to include. We recommend that if you are thinking about developing a large overall deck (from which you can select fifty to sixty cards to use at any one time) that you consider balancing three major variables: educational level; Holland's classification system; and the *Dictionary of Occupational Titles* classification system.

We suggest that you consider three educational groups:

Group A: Occupations usually requiring some high school, a high school degree, or high school plus some short-term additional training (forty to sixty cards)

Group B: Occupations usually requiring postsecondary education and training (forty to sixty cards)

Group C: Occupations usually requiring a college degree or postgraduate work (forty to sixty cards)

In addition, the occupations chosen for the overall card sort should include representation from each of Holland's (1979) personality and environmental types. As stated previously, the six types are described as follows:

Realistic	Involves working with tools, animals, or in an outdoor setting
Investigative	Involves investigating, understanding, and solving problems
Artistic	Involves use of imagination and creativity to make new ideas
Social	Involves helping, informing, and training people
Enterprising	Involves influencing, persuading, and managing people
Conventional	Involves working with data, numbers, and carrying out details

Holland's theory states that by comparing a person's attributes to each model type we can determine which type the individual resembles most. Since no individual totally resembles one type alone, we also determine to what extent the individual resembles the other types. The two or three types that the individual most resembles describe that person's code. For example, a person who is a counselor might have the code SAE, which indicates that this person resembles the social type the most, and the artistic and enterprising types to lesser degrees (in descending order). A bricklayer's pattern might be RCS, indicating resemblances to the realistic, conventional, and social types.

The codes are most easily understood using Holland's hexagonal model (Holland, 1979). The hexagon with the first letter of each type looks like this:

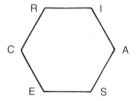

Types that are adjacent to each other on the hexagon are more similar than the types directly across from each other. S is more similar to A and E than it is to R. Codes consisting of closely related types occur more frequently than those that do not. For example, codes such as ESC and RIC occur more frequently than codes such as CSI and IES.

Finally, the occupations chosen for the overall card sort should include a mix of occupations representing various major categories of the *Dictionary of Occupational Titles* (1977). Approximately 20,000 occupations are classified, which are assigned a nine-digit code. For example, the occupation of the counselor has the following nine-digit code: 045. 107-010. The occupational group to which the counselor is assigned is identified by the first three-digit set (045). The second three-digit set refers to the worker function rating, or the counselor's relationship to data (1), people (0), and things (7). In *Dictionary* terminology this means that in their work, counselors have a coordinating relationship with data, a mentoring relationship with people, and a handling relationship with things. The lower the number, the more complex the relationship. The last three-digit set gives the alphabetical position of the occupational title within the six-digit code groups. The full nine-digit code number provides each occupation with its own unique code suitable for computerized operation.

So far we have suggested that educational level, Holland's classification system, and the *Dictionary of Occupational Titles* receive major consideration when you are developing your own card sort. There are other variables that you may need to consider depending on geographic and economic conditions. You may be living in an area where the local labor market is dominated by a certain business or industry. Also, rural/urban differences may be substantial in your area. In addition, the general state of the nation's economy may have an effect on the labor market, and the number of openings in various businesses and industries may fluctuate. It is not recommended, however, that local or regional situations completely dominate the selection of occupations in your card sort. Remember that a major goal of the card sort is to explore the theme system of your clients; it is not designed to be a job selection device, although it may function that way occasionally with some clients.

The cards for your own occupational card sort can be developed by following these steps.

1. Decide on the occupational titles you will use in your card sort.
2. Look up the title you have chosen and any alternate titles the job may be known by in the *Dictionary of Occupational Titles* (DOT). If you do not have a DOT, check with your local school, library, or state employment office. Read the description for each title you look up and note the DOT number.
3. When you have found the occupation descriptions that best match the occupational titles you have chosen, choose the title for that occupation with which most people would be familiar. If another title is used as frequently as the first or if the title under which the description is found is an obscure one, choose this second title as an alternate. Record the DOT number for the occupation description you have chosen.
4. Using the occupational description from the DOT and the description of the occupation from the *Occupational Outlook Handbook* (1984), write a brief, condensed description of the occupation.
5. Use the information regarding education and training requirements for these occupations found in the *Occupational Outlook Handbook* (1984) to write a condensed statement for each card.
6. The Holland code for the title can be determined by consulting Holland's *Occupations Finder* (1977). The 1979 edition of the *Professional Manual* (Holland, 1979) for the *Self-Directed Search* is helpful, as is the *Dictionary of Holland Occupational Codes* (1982).
7. Where possible, determine related occupations. Use titles from the same DOT group, or titles from the same industry, or titles commonly known to be related.
8. Once you have assembled the information from the above steps, print or type it onto 3 × 5 cards.

Each occupational card in your deck should have the same format. On the front of each card place the occupational title and an alternative title where applicable. On the back of each card put the brief description of the occupation. The education or training required is summarized and is also placed on the back of each card followed by a list of related occupations. In addition, the *Dictionary of Occupational Titles* number and the Holland (1979) three-letter code for that occupation should be placed in the upper right-hand and left-hand corners, respectively. Keeping the front of the cards free of all information other than occupational titles helps clients from being distracted as they sort the cards.

You will note that we recommend 3 × 5 cards. It has been our experience that this size is large enough to record sufficient information and yet small enough for clients to manipulate easily. Also, the size print possible

BOOKKEEPER

Conventional (CSI)   **210.382-018**

Maintains records in journals, ledgers, and accounting forms; prepares financial statements; analyzes and records all transactions, balances accounts, and calculates payrolls

High school required; business courses at junior colleges or business schools preferred

Account-information clerk, bookkeeping machine operator, credit card clerk, payroll clerk, reconcilement clerk

---

on a 3 × 5 card is large enough for most people to read with minimum difficulty.

So far, we have discussed an occupational card sort containing occupations representing various educational levels, Holland's types, and the DOT groupings. You may wish to develop a card sort that features specific occupational groupings, particularly if you work with special populations. If you are a personnel worker or career development specialist in business or industry, you may wish to develop a card sort built around the career ladders in your business or industry. Or you may wish to focus on a card sort that deals with motivation, job satisfaction, or values. As the saying goes, we are limited only by our imagination as to what is possible.

USING AN OCCUPATIONAL CARD SORT

Once you have developed your own card sort or have decided that it is more economical to purchase one that is commercially available, the next step is to consider the use of the card sort with your clients. If you purchase a commercially available sort, read the manual carefully. Whether you develop your own card sort or buy one, here are some ways to use a card sort. The Missouri Occupational Preference Inventory (MOPI, 1980)* is used here to illustrate the use of an occupational card sort. It contains 180 occupational cards. What follows is a description of the steps involved in using the MOPI. These steps may be similar to those used in other card sorts.

Getting Started

After you have chosen an appropriate grouping of cards for your client from the 180 cards in the MOPI, you will need to prepare your client and the setting before getting started. Also, depending on the population with which you work, you may find that one particular grouping of cards works well. Should you find a satisfactory grouping, keep it separate from the rest of the cards. By doing this, you will save yourself the effort of putting the cards back in order every time. If you are going to use one of the educational groupings, you will need to find out from your clients the amount of education or training they have or are willing to obtain in the next few years.

The group A MOPI cards consist of occupations that require some high school, a high school diploma, or high school plus some additional training. If you are working with an individual who is at this level and does not have plans to go any further in the next few years, this group would be appropriate. However, if the individual would like to explore occupations requiring more education, group B cards would be appropriate. They consist of occupations for which the education or training typically required is a postsecondary education or additional training. The additional training might be on-the-job, technical/vocational, junior college, or apprenticeship. This group is appropriate for individuals desiring or having this amount of training or education. It is not intended for those who wish to pursue a four-year degree in the next few years. Group C cards represent occupations that usually require a college degree or a postgraduate degree. This group is appropriate for individuals who wish to pursue or already have an advanced degree.

If the individual with whom you are working seems to be undecided about education or training, cards from each educational level can be used. For an even representation of occupations, twenty to twenty-five cards from each group can be chosen at random. If possible, we suggest that the initial deck you use with your clients contain occupations from each of

* Adapted from Earl Moore and Norman Gysbers with Pamela M. Carlson, *Missouri Occupational Preference Inventory Manual* (Columbia, Mo.: Human Systems Consultants, Inc., 1980, 110 N. Tenth St.). Used with permission.

Holland's types. If your client's Holland three-letter code is known, you may wish to include in your initial deck a majority of occupations from those categories. If the individual with whom you are working has indicated a desire to examine particular types of occupations, the DOT code may be useful for presorting purposes. For example, some individuals may prefer professional, technical, and managerial occupations, while others may prefer clerical and sales occupations.

Setting Arrangement

Find a place where you and your client can work undisturbed. You will need a table or desk. Arrange the card sort materials so that you sit next to one another rather than across from one another. This arrangement will facilitate the communication between the two of you. It also will help if there are worksheets to fill out and discuss.

Sorting the Cards

Before you have your client sort the cards that have been selected based on what you know about your client, make sure you fully explain the card sort process. Then the client will know what to expect and will probably be able to react in a more relaxed manner. You will want to emphasize that the major focus is not to select the right occupation, but rather to help explore the client's themes about self, others, and the world. Based on this information, discussion about future occupational selection or job changes can follow.

To begin the process you can use the following instructions:

Place the three choice cards in front of you from left to right as follows. Next look at each one of the occupational title cards.

For each card, decide whether you would like that occupation or dislike it. Place it below the appropriate choice cards. You may be undecided about some of the occupational cards. Put these cards below the undecided choice card. For all of the occupational cards assume that you have the ability for the occupation. The occupational titles in the like pile will be occupations you might actually choose, that have some specific appeal to you, or that seem appropriate for you. The occupational titles in the dislike pile will be occupations you are not interested in, you would not choose, or do not seem appropriate for a person like you. The occupational titles in the undecided pile will be those occupations you have both likes and dislikes for, or you are not sure if you would like them.

Begin sorting the occupations cards into three piles. Feel free to switch cards from one pile to another if you change your mind. Read the occupational description on the back of the card if you do not know what the particular occupation is. By doing this, it may help you to better decide whether you like or dislike that occupation.

Allow your clients time to work at their own pace. This includes allowing them time to read the occupational descriptions on the back of the cards, if necessary. It also is important for some clients to switch occupations from one pile to another. If clients feel rushed, they will not take the time to read a description or change their mind.

Sometimes clients will sort a large number of cards into the dislike pile. This indicates one of two things. First, it may mean that it is easier for them to indicate dislikes than likes. Second, a large proportion of cards in the dislike pile may mean they have been given an incorrect grouping of cards, for example, if a college student were given a group A set of cards. It is unlikely that this individual will have very many cards in the like pile.

Determining Reasons or Themes

After your client has sorted the appropriate grouping of cards, the next step is to talk about reasons behind choosing or not choosing a particular occupation. Individuals often are not aware of the reasons behind their choices or why they like or dislike an occupation. Becoming more aware of the reasons behind likes and dislikes will help them identify the themes that guide their life-styles.

Help your client get started in theme identification by reading or paraphrasing the following instructions. In the sample instructions that follow there is an example of occupational choices and the possible reasons for these choices. You can point out that often there is more than one reason for liking an occupation.

In order to better consider the reasons (themes) for choosing certain occupational titles, begin by thinking about the first occupational card in the like pile. Explain the reason or reasons why you like it. Do this for each card in the like pile. Make sure each reason is specific. For example, if working with people is a reason, what specifically do you like? Would you prefer working with people by instructing, persuading, leading, or being led by them? Another example might be working with objects or things. What kinds of things? Do you prefer office machines, tools, factory assembly, or heavy equipment? Some examples for liking certain occupations might be:

OCCUPATIONAL TITLES	REASON
Physician, psychologist, lawyer	Prestigious
Physician, engineer	Pays well
Lawyer, insurance broker	Working with people, persuading

Sometimes an occupational title will stimulate two or more reasons. For example, the reasons for choosing physician may be "prestige" and "pays well." Now, begin giving reasons for choices in the like pile.

If your client has difficulty and cannot describe any reasons, explore the reasons behind a particular choice. Questions such as the following will help your client explore:

- What attracts you to this occupation?
- What parts of it would you like best?
- Would you enjoy the opportunity to work with numbers (people, heavy equipment, or whatever is appropriate)?
- Would you like it because you're indoors (or outdoors)?

Questions such as these usually will help your client get started. Or you may be able to personalize the discussion by briefly telling about your reasons for liking a particular occupation.

As your client identifies reasons, write the reasons in the like column on a worksheet divided into three columns as presented below.

FINDING THEMES

Likes	Dislikes	Undecided
		+ −

Place a slash mark next to the reason. For each reason mentioned again, add another slash mark. In this way, a running total can be kept for every reason mentioned. For example, the like column on the "Finding Themes" worksheet might look like this:

FINDING THEMES

Likes	Dislikes	Undecided
Prestigious 11		+ −
Pays well ⅬⱧⱵ		
Working with people 1		
(teaching)		

The next step is to have your client identify the reasons for placing occupational titles in the dislike pile and in the undecided pile.

Now, think about the cards in the dislike pile and explain the reasons for not choosing these occupations.

If there are any cards in the undecided pile, think about these once again. These occupations may stimulate both negative and positive descriptions. Explain why you are undecided about each occupation in this pile.

The reasons mentioned for placing the cards in the dislike pile are recorded in the dislike column on the "Finding Themes" worksheet in the same manner that the likes were recorded. The dislike column might look like this:

FINDING THEMES

Likes	Dislikes	Undecided
	Working with machines 1111	+ −
	Menial work 1111	
	Too much structure 1	

If the individual has cards in the undecided pile, these can be discussed next. If the reason has already been recorded in the like or dislike column, another slash mark is placed by it. If it is a reason that has not been mentioned yet, record it in the undecided column, a positive reason under the plus sign (+) and a negative reason under the negative sign (−).

The next step in the process of determining reasons or themes involves using the "Understanding Themes," worksheet. On this worksheet the reasons or themes that were identified on the "Finding Themes" worksheet are rank ordered. To review quickly, the completed "Finding Themes" worksheet from our previous example was filled out as follows:

FINDING THEMES

Likes	Dislikes	Undecided
Prestigious 11	Working with machines 1111	+ −
Pays well ⊥⊦⊦⊤	Menial work 1111	
Working with people 1 (teaching)	Too much structure 1	

On the "Understanding Themes" worksheet the reasons or themes are rank ordered. By ranking these reasons, priorities can be established. The first step is to rank order the reasons in the like column. These should be in order from the greatest number of slash marks to those with the fewest. This is how the "Understanding Themes" worksheet will begin to look:

UNDERSTANDING THEMES

Likes	Dislikes
Pays well	
Prestigious	
Working with people (teaching)	

After the likes have been rank ordered, you and your client can fill in the dislike column. Of the reasons mentioned for the dislike column, some of them will be direct opposites of the reasons mentioned in the like column. The reason in the example, "pays well," does not have an opposite; however, "prestigious" and "working with people (teaching)" do. The opposites for these, respectively, are "menial work" and "working with machines." This is how the worksheet should look now:

UNDERSTANDING THEMES

Likes	Dislikes
Pays well	
Prestigious	Menial work
Working with people (teaching)	Working with machines
	Too much structure
	Outdoor work

You will notice that "too much structure" and "outdoor work" were also mentioned as dislikes. Even though these reasons don't have direct opposites in the like column, they are still included, but on lines just below the other dislikes. If there are likes and dislikes in the undecided column, fill these in also under an undecided column.

To complete the worksheet, fill in reasons for which there are not direct opposites. You can do this by asking your client what the opposites are. The purpose of filling in opposites is to find out more about the reasons behind your client's choices. In the above examples, "indoor work," "independent," and "doesn't pay well" were not mentioned as original reasons; however, this part of the step brings them into focus. A focus on opposites may result in insight for your client. The following is an example of what the worksheet might look like when it is completed:

UNDERSTANDING THEMES

Likes	Dislikes
Pays well	Doesn't pay well
Prestigious	Menial work
Working with people (teaching)	Working with machines
Independent	Too much structure
Indoor work	Outdoor work

In this example the individual responded with "doesn't pay well" as an opposite of "pays well." "Independent" was the opposite of "too much structure" and "indoor work" was the opposite of "outdoor work." Sometimes your client may not have an opposite. It is not necessary to fill one in if your client does not have one.

At this point you may wish to spend some time discussing the reasons or themes with your client. This is an optional step; however, if you have the time it can be beneficial. Here are some examples of some types of questions you could ask:

1. Explain what meaning each of the reasons has for you.
2. If you could not have an ideal job with all the reasons listed, which two or three would you have to have?
3. Describe someone you know who has a job with some or all of the reasons listed.

Some individuals will be able to discuss their reasons spontaneously, while others will need more structure. Question 1 above may need more structure than the last two questions. Questions to facilitate that discussion might be:

1. Explain what meaning each of the reasons has for you.
   - "Pays well" means one thing to one person and another to someone else. What would be good pay and what would be considered poor pay for you?
   - Does "indoor work" mean never being outdoors?
   - Who do you know who has a "prestigious" job? What about the job makes it important and valued?
   - For the reason "working with people (teaching)," what kinds of subjects, with what age group, and with what sort of population?
   - How "independent" would you like to be? Do you want to be your own boss or would you prefer to have a boss that likes some structure but not a lot?

Ranking Occupations

The next step in the process involves asking your client to rank order occupational preferences using the like pile. Begin by reading or paraphrasing the following instructions to your client.

Now that you know more about the reasons behind your occupational choices, rank order them. Look at the cards in the like pile again. Decide which one would be your first choice, your second choice, and so on, for all the occupations that seem to be important to you.

Most people rank order from seven to twelve occupations. If two occupations are close in ranking, you can suggest that your client try to order them as well as possible. After your client has prioritized the occupations, ask him or her to read to you the occupational titles and their three-letter Holland codes. Suppose your client rank ordered the following seven occupations. The ranking and the Holland code listing would look like this.

PRIORITIZING OCCUPATIONAL PREFERENCES

Occupational Title	Holland Code
Landscape architect	RIA
Optician	ISR
Economist	IAS
Jeweler	RIS
Contractor	ERI
Real estate agent	ECS
Public relations representative	AES

These Holland codes can be used to derive a summary code to help your client gain a greater understanding of self. The number of letters in each column are counted and applied to the formula that follows, which yields the summary code. The first part of the computation requires you to total the number of R's, I's, A's, S's, E's, and C's. Using the letters in the sample "Prioritizing Occupational Preferences" worksheet, count all of the R's in the first column. Then count all of the I's and so on until every letter (if it appears) has been counted. The same procedure is used for the second and third columns. Here are the results of the counting for the sample worksheet above.

PRIORITIZING OCCUPATIONAL PREFERENCES

	Col. 1	Col. 2	Col. 3
R's	2	1	1
I's	2	2	1
A's	1	1	1
S's	0	1	4
E's	2	1	0
C's	0	1	0

As you count the number of letters, fill them in on the "Finding Your Summary Holland Code" worksheet.

FINDING YOUR SUMMARY HOLLAND CODE

1st Letter	2nd Letter	3rd Letter	Total
R ___ × 3 = ☐	___ × 2 = ☐	___ × 1 = ☐ = ___	
I ___ × 3 = ☐	___ × 2 = ☐	___ × 1 = ☐ = ___	
A ___ × 3 = ☐	___ × 2 = ☐	___ × 1 = ☐ = ___	
S ___ × 3 = ☐	___ × 2 = ☐	___ × 1 = ☐ = ___	
E ___ × 3 = ☐	___ × 2 = ☐	___ × 1 = ☐ = ___	
C ___ × 3 = ☐	___ × 2 = ☐	___ × 1 = ☐ = ___	

The worksheet would now look like this.

1st Letter	2nd Letter	3rd Letter	Total
R _2_ × 3 = ☐	_1_ × 2 = ☐	_1_ × 1 = ☐ = ___	
I _2_ × 3 = ☐	_2_ × 2 = ☐	_1_ × 1 = ☐ = ___	
A _1_ × 3 = ☐	_1_ × 2 = ☐	_1_ × 1 = ☐ = ___	
S _0_ × 3 = ☐	_1_ × 2 = ☐	_4_ × 1 = ☐ = ___	
E _2_ × 3 = ☐	_1_ × 2 = ☐	_0_ × 1 = ☐ = ___	
C _0_ × 3 = ☐	_1_ × 2 = ☐	_0_ × 1 = ☐ = ___	

After you have filled in the numbers, do the multiplication, putting the answers in the boxes. Next, total the numbers in the boxes and write the answer in the "Total" column. A completed worksheet is shown on p. 146. This first letter of the summary code will be the highest number in the "Total" column; the second letter will be the second highest number and the third letter, the third highest.

The summary code in the example is IRE. Errors in the computation can happen, so make certain that the code is correct by rechecking it. Occasionally there will be ties. In the event there is a tie for the third-letter place, use four letters. If, for example, the "Total" column reads R = 9, I = 11, S = 8, E = 8, C = 2, the summary code would be IRS/E.

It is suggested that when ties occur for places other than third, only

Total

R 2 × 3 = 6   1 × 2 = 2   1 × 1 = 1 = 9

I 2 × 3 = 6   2 × 2 = 4   1 × 1 = 1 = 11

A 1 × 3 = 3   1 × 2 = 2   1 × 1 = 1 = 6

S 0 × 3 = 0   1 × 2 = 2   4 × 1 = 4 = 6

E 2 × 3 = 6   1 × 2 = 2   0 × 1 = 0 = 8

C 0 × 3 = 0   1 × 2 = 2   0 × 1 = 0 = 2

three letters be used, not four. If there is a tie for first place, assign the letters to second and third place. Assignment of the letters to specific places is not crucial and can be somewhat arbitrary, because various combinations of the three-letter code is used in the actual exploration of occupations. It should be noted that, depending on the distribution of the numbers, the above recommendations may not hold. In these cases exercise your judgment.

After the code is computed and checked, review the Holland system of classification with your client. A description of the code can be made at this point or in the next step. It is necessary to find out if the code makes sense to your client. In most cases individuals will agree that the description of each type in their code applies to them. If not, discuss why the code does not make sense. Remember, your task is not to classify or label, your task is to help clients explore self-perceptions as they may relate to card sort data.

Helping Your Client Summarize the Card Sort Data

The summarization portion of the card sort process is intended to help your client focus on what has been learned. The "Your Career Information Summary" worksheet that follows can be used in this step. It consists of:

- Summarizing the themes
- Recording the top five occupations
- Recording the summary Holland code
- Describing the code for your client
- Formulating a plan of action

The accompanying worksheet gives structure to the summarization process as well as the opportunity to help plan your client's future steps.

YOUR CAREER INFORMATION SUMMARY

Name _____ Date _____

Themes (summarize from the "Understanding Themes" worksheet)

_____

_____

_____

Occupations (Top five from "Prioritizing Occupational Preferences" worksheet)

Top Five	DOT	Holland Code
_____	___ __ ___	_____
_____	___ __ ___	_____
_____	___ __ ___	_____
_____	___ __ ___	_____
_____	___ __ ___	_____

Summary Holland Code _____ _____ _____

Holland Types

Realistic — People who have athletic or mechanical ability. They prefer to work outside with their hands with tools, machines, plants, or animals rather than with ideas or people.

Investigative — People who like to solve problems that require thinking. They enjoy working with ideas and words, especially centering around science.

Artistic — People who have artistic, innovative, or intuitional abilities. They like work in unstructured situations using their imagination or creativity.

Social — People who like to work with people and are good with words. They like to inform, teach, help, and train others.

Enterprising — People who are good at talking and using words to persuade, influence, and manage for organizational or economic goals.

Conventional — People who like to work with data and have clerical or numerical ability. They prefer to follow others' directions and carry out activities in detail.

Plan of Action (steps)

1. _____

2. _____

3. _____

4. _____

5. _____

In order to complete the worksheet, begin by summarizing the themes. You can ask your clients to summarize in their own words what themes are most important to them. If your clients are unable to do this or have difficulty with it, you can summarize the themes as you see them.

CLIENT 1 (A 23-Year-Old Man)

Understanding Themes

Likes	Dislikes
Exciting	Boring
Meeting different people	Working by myself
Creating with hands	Not using hands
Helping people	No contact with people
Travel	Staying in one place
Pays well	Pays lousy
Man's job	Woman's job
Prestigious work	Dirty work, low job

SUMMARIZATION

Themes (summarize from **Understanding Themes**)

In a job I would like to be able to keep busy with people and to be able to consider my job a worthwhile job and to be able to like what I am doing.

CLIENT 2 (A 33-Year-Old Woman)

Understanding Themes

Likes	Dislikes
Instructing people	Supervising
Creative	Dull
Contributing, seeing results	Not seeing results
Working with food	
Activity	Rigid activity (desk job)

SUMMARIZATION

Themes (summarize from **Understanding Themes**)

I prefer to work in an active and stimulating environment with a variety of people; being able to see directly the results of my efforts. I would like to be in charge on a limited level and learn new things while I work.

Check to see if they agree or disagree with your summary. Either you or your clients can write down the summary in the space provided. The two examples that follow illustrate the use of the "Understanding Themes" worksheet to help summarize themes. As you will see, there is no "right" answer against which to judge a summary.

The next part of the "Your Career Information Summary" worksheet involves filling in the top five occupations from the "Prioritizing Occupational Preferences" worksheet. These may be occupations that your client may want to explore further. If your client wishes to explore them further, include the DOT number and Holland code for exploration purposes. Next, write in the summary Holland code in the space provided. If you have not discussed the code with your client yet, do so at this point. Remember, it is important to find out if the code makes sense.

The last step in filling out the "Your Career Information Summary" worksheet involves making some plans for the future. Most individuals will want to work on some next steps. Ask your clients what they might want to do. Depending on the response, you may want to make some additional suggestions. If they do not know what the future plans might include, offer some suggestions. When making suggestions, be sure to gain agreement with your clients. In some cases, they may not want to make future plans. Explore this with them. It may indicate they do not know what steps to take or that they are not ready to make plans.

SOME CLOSING THOUGHTS

Now that you have had a chance to read about an occupational card sort, let us review briefly some of its uses with your clients. As you have seen, it is a technique that can help evoke a word picture of your client's themes. It does this by providing stimuli to help you and your clients evoke a picture of who they are and how they view others and the world in which they live. The evoking process is prompted by asking clients to give reasons for choices and various groupings of occupations. Occupational titles are the common everyday terms that supply the stimuli while the card sort process supplies the setting for the process to unfold. This process is similar to that which was anticipated by Pritchard over twenty years ago when he wrote:

> Particular occupational stimili should be selected and used, with the counselee's participation, for their apparent specific utilities (as in the case of tests) in helping to elicit, explore, and clarify his needs, values, attitudes, aspirations, expectations, and work-role and self perceptions." (Pritchard, 1962, p. 667)

An occupational card sort has the potential of helping cilents explore career options. In effect, an occupational card sort and the process involved in using it provide a springboard for further educational and occupational exploration. It does so by providing points of entry into various occupational classification systems such as the DOT and Holland codes, by giving clients lists of related occupations to help them broaden their perspective about what might be possible, and by presenting education and training requirements. The point of entry use is enhanced by the *Dictionary of Holland Occupational Codes* (Gottfredson, Holland, and Ogawa, 1982). This is a cross-index of Holland's RIASEC codes with the 12,099 occupational base titles of the DOT. It also provides information about the general educational development (GED) and the specific vocational preparation (SVP) for each of the occupations.

The occupational card sort process described in this chapter is the process used with the Missouri Occupational Preference Inventory (Moore and Gysbers, 1980). Although most occupational card sort processes are similar, each of the published ones will have their own approaches. Thus it is necessary to read the manuals for the card sorts carefully.

If you decide that the card sort process is a technique that you would find helpful in career counseling, we recommend that you first consider purchasing one of the published card sorts since it will save you time. For more information, refer to the National Vocational Guidance Association's *A Counselor's Guide to Vocational Guidance Instruments* (Kapes and Mastie, 1982), which has a section that reviews some of the currently available card sorts. Addresses of the publishers also are provided. On the other hand, developing your own card sort may make sense because of the population you are serving or the labor market in which you work. You will find the work involved is not too difficult. In fact, in some situations clients can assist in developing the appropriate cards.

REFERENCES

COOPER, J. F., "Comparative Impact of the SCII and the Vocational Card Sort on the Career Salience and Career Exploration of Women," *Journal of Counseling Psychology*, 23 (1976), 348–52.
DEWEY, C. R., "Exploring Interests: A Non-Sexist Method." *Personnel and Guidance Journal*, 52 (1974), 311–15.
DOLLIVER, R. H., "An Adaptation of the Tyler Vocational Card Sort," *Personnel and Guidance Journal*, 45 (1967), 916–20.
———, "Card Sorts," in *A Counselor's Guide to Vocational Guidance Instruments*, eds. J. T. Kapes and M. M. Mastie. Washington D.C.: National Vocational Guidance Association, 1982.
———, and WILL, J. A., "Ten-year Follow-Up of the Tyler Vocational Card Sort and the Strong Vocational Interest Blank," *Journal of Counseling Psychology*, 24 (1977), 48–54.
EDMONDS, T., "Applying Personal Construct Theory in Occupational Guidance," *British Journal of Guidance and Counselling*, 7, no. 2 (1979).
GOTTFREDSON, G. D., HOLLAND, J. L., and OGAWA, D. K., *Dictionary of Holland Occupational Codes*. Palo Alto, Calif.: Consulting Psychologists Press, 1982.
HOLLAND, J. L., *The Occupations Finder*. Palo Alto, Calif.: Consulting Psychologists Press, 1977.
———, *The Self-Directed Search Professional Manual* (1979 ed.). Palo Alto, Calif.: Consulting Psychologists Press, 1979.

JONES, L. K., "Occu-Sort: Development and Evaluation of an Occupational Card Sort System," *The Vocational Guidance Quarterly*, 28 (1979), 56–62.

———, "Issues in Developing an Occupational Card Sort," *Measurement and Evaluation in Guidance*, 12, no. 4 (1980), 206–15.

———, "A Comparison of Two Self-Directed Career Guidance Instruments: Occu-Sort and Self-Directed Search," *The School Counselor*, 30, no. 3 (1983).

KAPES, J. T., and MASTIE, M. M., eds., *A Counselor's Guide to Vocational Guidance Instruments*. Washington D.C.: National Vocational Guidance Association, 1982.

KNOWDELL, R. L. *Career Assessment Instruments*. San Jose, Calif.: Career Research and Testing, 1982.

MOORE, E. J., and GYSBERS, N. C., *Missouri Occupational Preference Inventory*. Columbia, Mo.: Human Systems Consultants, Inc., 1980.

PRITCHARD, D. H., "The Occupational Exploration Process: Some Operational Implications," *Personnel and Guidance Journal*, 40, no. 8 (1962).

TYLER, L. E., "Research Explorations in the Realm of Choice," *Journal of Counseling Psychology*, 8 (1961).

U.S. Department of Labor, *Dictionary of Occupational Titles* (4th ed.). Washington, D.C.: U.S. Government Printing Office, 1977.

———, *Occupational Outlook Handbook* (1984–85 ed.). Washington, D.C.: U.S. Government Printing Office, 1984.

CHAPTER **6**

Individual
Career Plans

*Our task is to teach people the skills they need to manage their
own careers. That doesn't mean telling people what occupations
they ought to pursue; nor does it mean we tell them what
education they should get. . . . What it does mean is that we
give them data—data about themselves, data about technology,
data about the economy, data about demographic trends, data
about employers—all the data we can gather that in any way
impacts upon their vocational lives and choices—and we teach
them how to use those data to manage their own careers.
(Wilhelm, 1983, p. 12)*

Once a client's goal or problem has been identified,
clarified, and specified, the next step is the resolution of the goal or problem. In the career counseling framework this is called the taking action
phase. It is the point when interventions based on your diagnoses are
begun. Counseling techniques, testing, personal styles analyses, and career
and labor market information are examples of typical interventions widely
used in career counseling today.

Chapter 6 introduces another intervention for you to consider, the
individual career plan. Individual career plans can be thought of as both
instruments and processes that individuals can use alone or with the help of
others to monitor and carry forward their career development. As instruments, plans can provide places to organize and record the aptitudes, abilities, interests, values, and skills indentified during career assessment and
counseling. They can become organizers for personal, education, and career and labor market information, which then can be updated periodi-
cally. As processes, plans can become pathways or guides through which
individuals can use the past and present to look forward to the future.
They can become vehicles for planning.

Chapter 6 begins by describing the essential characteristics of an individual career plan. Then possible structures for a plan are presented.* These include a comprehensive plan built around life roles and two plans that focus on the worker role. The chapter closes with some concluding remarks about the development and use of individual career plans with clients.

PLAN CHARACTERISTICS

Before we describe and discuss three different types of individual career plans for possible use with clients, it is important to consider some essential plan characteristics. We recommend that a plan, regardless of format, be comprehensive, developmental, person centered and person directed, and competency based.

Comprehensive

An individual career plan should be a guide to help people manage change in their lives. It should help them define their goals and identify and expand their aptitudes, abilities, interests, values, and skills. It should be a record, never completed, of their past, present, and future experiences and goals. A plan should provide a way, in written form, for people to identify and consider who they are, where they are going, and how they are going to get there in terms of life roles such as worker, consumer/citizen, learner, personal, and family member.

Developmental

An individual career plan should be designed to be used throughout the life span. It should be a document that is always in a state of change. Thus it should contain elements that are responsive to the demands and challenges of different life roles and stages. Although it can be used on a one-time basis, it should be a flexible document that can be filled out and modified from time to time as new experiences are anticipated or completed.

Person Centered and Person Directed

Individual career plans should belong to the people using them. Plans should not be the property of institutions, businesses, industries, or agencies, although they may be kept in these setttings for convenience if the individuals involved are working or participating in programs in these

* Adapted from N. C. Gysbers, *Create and Use an Individual Career Development Plan* (Columbus, Ohio: National Center for Research in Vocational Education, published and distributed by Bell & Howell Publication Systems Division, Wooster, Ohio, 1985). Used with permission.

settings. Also, while a plan, by definition, is a personal document, many people, including business and industry personnel, teachers, counselors, and agency staff members, should be involved in how a plan is created and how it unfolds. However, the fact remains, a plan should remain person centered and person directed.

Competency Based

Personal aptitudes, interests, and values are important elements in the development of individual career plans. So, too, is consideration of past and present experiences and achievements. To these possible plan elements should be added the idea of competencies. Competencies are skills, knowledge, and attitudes individuals acquire as they learn, work, and live in such settings as home, school, workplace, and community. An individual career plan should have a component that provides an opportunity to identify and record current competencies and that helps indicate what additional competencies may be needed to respond to future life role needs and challenges.

PLAN STRUCTURES

Up to now we have not dealt with the question of what individual career plans should look like. Although specific answers to this question depend on the needs of the clients with whom you work, we would like to suggest three different types of plans that you and your clients might consider. The first plan uses life roles as an organizer and is called the comprehensive career plan. The second and third plans focus specifically on the worker role and are called the career portfolio and career passport, respectively.

Life Roles—Comprehensive Career Plan

The life roles of worker, consumer/citizen, learner, personal, and family member are used to provide the main section of this plan. The structure for this plan can be a three-ring binder or a folder with various inserts. A booklet form also can be used. With the increasing availability and use of microcomputers consideration also can be given to adapting this plan to computer use. Perhaps some combination of paper and pencil and computer might work best. The computer can store information for easy retrieval and the notebook or folder can be used for laying out and monitoring action steps. We see the possibility of being able to retrieve information about one's home, insurance policies, health, work record, taxes, family, educational experiences, volunteer opportunities, test data, investments, and so forth at a moment's notice and then use that information to make decisions about next steps.

The main section of this plan is organized around these major headings:

- Worker role
- Consumer/citizen role
- Learner role
- Personal role
- Family member role

In the life-role section of the notebook or folder individuals can record a wide range of information. The following section presents a few ideas about the topics of information that can be collected and recorded for each of the life roles.

Worker Role.   In this section individuals record information about the worker role competencies they possess. A listing of interest and aptitude data also can be included. In addition, tasks performed around home or school and the jobs individuals have had can be recorded.

Consumer/Citizen Role.   This section of a plan includes individuals' competencies identified in this role. Special attention is given to listings of community resources used or those that are available to be used. Depending on the age of the persons involved, information is recorded concerning the purchase and maintenance of housing, the investment of money, and legal transactions including the establishment of funds and wills.

Learner Role.   In this section a complete record of the individual's educational experiences and achievements are recorded and maintained. Official transcripts, listings of learner competencies acquired, listings of informal learning experiences, and extracurricular activities are just a few of the types of learner role information that can be included.

Personal Role.   This section could be used by individuals to record and maintain information about themselves including their personal appearance, values, friendships, and leisure-time pursuits. In addition, this is the section to record and maintain complete health records. This can include immunizations received, medication taken, doctor or hospital visits, childhood diseases, and past illnesses.

Family Member Role.   The family member role section is used to record and maintain such information as family background, data about family members and relatives, and possible family crises and what was done to handle them. Other information that can be recorded and maintained are data about family milestones or important family-related occurrences such as marriages, divorces, illnesses, and birthdays. Short anecdotes about such occurrences also can be included.

Career Growth Action Steps. In addition to the main section with its focus on life roles, we suggest that this plan contain a section in which individuals can think through and lay out plans for career growth or future endeavors. This section of the plan provides the opportunity to analyze and synthesize information recorded in the life-role sections and to generalize these findings to present and future actions. More specifically, this section of a plan is where short-range and long-range goals are recorded and monitored and behavioral contracts with self and others are kept. Possible barriers to the completion of goals can be identified. Friendship and support groups can be noted and possible role models and mentors identified, listed, and contacted. Finally, specific action steps toward individual career growth are recorded and monitored in this section. For example, such action steps might list enrolling in a short-term training program to take advantage of a new job opening, reviewing the issues and steps involved in moving from one community to another to accept a new job, or thinking through and listing the activities involved in improving one's physical condition. These action steps (or any others, for that matter) may emerge after individuals have analyzed and synthesized the information recorded in the life-role sections of their plans.

Worker Role—the Career Portfolio

The life-roles structure for an individual career plan is designed for use in overall life career planning and decision making. This focus may be too broad for some clients and their needs. Some clients may need a plan structure that helps them organize and use self- and labor market information for the job hunt or for advancement or job-changing purposes. The career portfolio is designed to respond to this more specific need.

The career portfolio is designed to help individuals who are entering or reentering the labor market, considering advancement possibilities, or changing jobs to record and document the work, education and training, and personal experiences they have had and the skills they have acquired. The career portfolio is not a resumé. It is a personal repository for information from which clients can draw information for resumé writing, for filling out job applications, or for other job-hunting purposes.

The example career portfolio that follows has two sections. These sections are the job performance credential and the personal profile sheet.

Job Performance Credential. The job performance credential is divided into four main areas typically addressed on job applications: personal, education, work record, and primary job skills. What follows is an example of a job performance credential form and the guidelines for filling it out.

Personal Section. In this section clients list their name, social security number, address, and telephone number.

Education Section. Clients list education and training experiences in the education section, along with emphasis areas if applicable as well as any certificates or licenses. Additional information in this section might include job-related test scores. For example, individuals applying for a position as secretary might want to include their typing or shorthand proficiency scores since these would relate directly to employment and may not be recorded elsewhere.

Work Record Section. Clients list any work experience, volunteer experience, on-the-job training, or military experience.

Primary Job Skills Section. Clients list those skills that are specifically job related. For example, a person who has been a diesel mechanic or who has been trained in this occupation might list, "Troubleshoot diesel engines, fuel systems, and repair them," or "Describe and perform basic engine overhaul." Similarly, a person who has been an offset lithographer might list "Tear down and clear printing machines, reassemble them, and properly care for all other machinery in the print shop." In this section only skills that are job related are listed.

Personal Profile Sheet. The personal profile sheet is divided into four sections. The sections along with some ideas about what individuals could include are as follows:

Work Interests, Traits, and Attitudes. In this section individuals include the different types of work activity they have done and enjoy. These activities might include dealing with things and objects (repairing machinery), personal contact to help or instruct others (teaching, training), and communication of ideas or information (writing, speaking). In addition, they also could describe work-related traits and attitudes they feel they possess, such as being loyal, reliable, patient, organized, self-disciplined, willing to learn, and people oriented.

Special Training or Skills/Abilities. In this section are included any skills not mentioned as primary skills elsewhere, such as skills developed by individuals that are not necessarily job specific. For example, using my hands as in assembling, constructing, building, as with kits or carpentry; operating tools, machinery or equipment, as with drills, sewing machines, trucks, or lawn mowers; showing finger dexterity, handling with precision and repairing as in assembly line work, repairing autos, machines; using numbers as in taking inventory, calculating, keeping a checkbook.

JOB PERFORMANCE CREDENTIAL

<table>
<tr><td rowspan="3" style="vertical-align:middle">P E R S O N A L</td><td colspan="3">Name   Last   First   Middle initial   Social Security No.</td></tr>
<tr><td>Present address (street, city, state, zip)   Present phone area code</td></tr>
<tr><td>Permanent address   Permanent phone, area code</td></tr>
</table>

E D U C A T I O N	Schools attended (name/loc.)	Dates (mo./yr.) From To	Degree Earned	Grad. Mo.	Date Yr.	Speciality/ emphasis area

Additional information:

W O R K R E C O R D	Employment experience (included are permanent, volunteer, OJT, and U.S. military service)			
	Work experience (Name and address of employer)	Description of work (Descriptive title)	Hrs. per week	Dates (mo./yr.) From To

P R I M A R Y   J O B   S K I L L S

PERSONAL PROFILE

This page is an opportunity to give you and your potential employer a better idea of the personal qualities you possess that might lend themselves to success on the job. You are also encouraged to comment on how you personalize each of these activities. (What "pay-off" or "reward" do each of these activities hold for you personally?)

WORK INTERESTS, TRAITS, AND ATTITUDES

Include activities to help determine what types of work you are interested in and what positive work attitudes you have developed, such as being a self-starter, motivation toward learning new tasks, or assuming new responsibilities.

SPECIAL TRAINING OR SKILLS/ABILITIES NOT MENTIONED ELSEWHERE

Include activities that will help you display the skills and abilities you have developed in other areas of your experience.

FAVORITE CLASSES, SUBJECTS, AND SCHOOL ACTIVITIES

Include activities in school such as sports, awards, achievements, clubs, and vocational training, and favorite classes.

SOCIAL/LEISURE ACTIVITIES

Include your leisure-time activites such as community clubs, athletic teams, church activities, personal hobbies, and interests

Favorite Classes, Training Programs, Subjects, and Educational Activities. In this section individuals include formal school activities, awards, and achievements in addition to experiences in clubs, musical groups, drama groups, athletic teams, leadership roles, and so on.

Social/Leisure Activities. Activities the client enjoys doing in his or her spare time are listed in this section. Is a hobby pursued on a regular basis? (By hobby we refer to any activity that is special to the individual and indicates more than a passing interest in a particular area.) Is there participation in any organizations not connected with school? Are these organizations attended on a regular basis?

Worker Role—The Career Passport

Another, more specific type of individual career plan that you may want to use with some clients is a career passport. The career passport idea originated at the National Institute for Work and Learning as a part of a project to assist young people in documenting their prior experiences and in the employment interview (Barton, 1981). As Barton put it:

> Adults who are successful in finding jobs prepare for their interviews and usually carry a resumé with them. Youth have records of their *academic* experiences, which can be very important in securing a job, but have no comparable record of their other developmental experiences. Young people's infamiliarity with the employment interview and lack of documentation of their prior experience is a serious gap when they begin to look for a job. (Barton, 1981, p. 3)

While the focus of the career passport at the National Institute for Work and Learning was on young people, we see the potential in the concept for individuals of all ages. The career passport provides clients with a handy reference to organized information they may need for job interviews or for job applications, whether for entry-level first-time jobs or for midcareer job changing. It has some of the same information found in the career portfolio, but it also contains ideas and hints about how to use the career passport for personal assessment, how to fill out job applications, and how to conduct oneself during a job interview.

A sample career passport is given on the following pages. Depending on the experience, background, and level of sophistication of your clients, you could add to, subtract from, or modify the sample passport's format and content.

As you can see from the sample, the career passport provides clients with a way to think about themselves, their background, and their experiences. It also provides them with a place to record this information. It can be particularly helpful in building self-confidence and in improving the

Text continued on page 169.

CAREER PASSPORT

Name

Address

Telephone number

Social Security number

Knowing How To Get What You Want

Business invests heavily in improving their products and creating new ones. They research customer reaction to their products and learn what new products are wanted. Finding a job is similar to selling a product. You are selling your skills, talents, and abilities to the employer who can offer you the most opportunity. Viewing yourself as a business forces you to think about what you are selling.

Potential employers will be interested in knowing what you bring with you that will contribute to their organization's success. The more specific the information, the more useful it is. In order to effectively sell yourself, it is important that you have an effective way to present yourself. The most common mistake people make in making decisions about job opportunities is that they fail to consider all the relevant factors.

What Your Passport Can Do

During a job interview, you don't have time to plow through a pile of badly organized papers or poorly written notes about your qualifications and interests. The career passport can help you by:

- Organizing job-relevant information about you in a clear and understandable way.

- Focusing on how you can contribute to the employer's business.

- Developing a better understanding between you and the employer.

- Building a framework for resolving uncertainties, developing trust, and promoting straight talk.

Job Performance Credential

Developing and presenting a new improved you is as important as it is for all other businesses that want to stay competitive and grow. Your product is you—your ability to do the job. Your skills shape what your job will be and what it might become.

It is important that during an interview you be able to present yourself in the best possible light. This means being able to focus on your strongest selling points and answering questions in a straightforward, factual manner.

Time becomes a critical factor in an interview and the job performance credential makes important information readily available to you when you need it. It can also be extremely helpful as a reference when you are asked to fill out a job application since the information is similar to that commonly asked for by businesses.

Your career passport is divided into three major sections:

- JOB PERFORMANCE CREDENTIAL

- PERSONAL PROFILE

- INTERVIEWING TIPS

Information for completing the first two sections can be easily obtained from your most recent career portfolio.

JOB PERFORMANCE CREDENTIAL: RESUME

PERSONAL

Name _____ Soc. Sec. # _____

Address _____ Phone # _____ Date of birth ___ ___ ___

EDUCATIONAL

Schools attended _____ From _____ To _____ Graduated _____

_____ From _____ To _____ Graduated _____

_____ From _____ To _____ Graduated _____

Educational specialty or emphasis areas _____

_____

_____

OCCUPATION

Employment experience (permanent, volunteer, OJT and military service). List most recent position first:

Employer   Address   Position   Hrs. per week   From/To   Supervisor

_____

Primary job skills (skills specifically related to job being applied for):

_____

References will be furnished upon request.

165

Personal Profile

The ability to take charge of your career is one part of personal growth. Personal growth is a big idea. It means reaching for satisfaction and development in all aspects of your life. The job you take will become a major source of your growth. It is important that you be able to assess and present those qualities you have which make you the right person for the job. This information will give the employer a better idea of whether you are the person that he or she is looking for as well as allow you to decide if this is a job you can be satisfied with. There is a decided advantage in knowing "who you are" before going into a job interview. The personal profile can provide you a handy reference for discussing your personal qualities with a prospective employer.

Questions Employers May Ask

The following are a brief sample of questions that you may expect to be asked during a job interview. Review these questions carefully and consider how you might answer each of them.

Use the job performance credential and also the personal profile on the next page to help you with your answers.

Did you enjoy school?

What did you like best about it? Least? Why?

What school activities did you participate in?

What position are you interested in?

Why are you interested in this job?

Have you ever done this type of work before?

What other jobs have you had? Have you had any volunteer experience?

Tell me about the work you did on your last job and what you liked about it?

What skills do you have? What tools, equipment or machines can you operate?

What qualifications do you have that will help you do this job successfully?

Why do you think you would like to work for us?

PERSONAL PROFILE

Work interests, traits, and attitude: _____

_____

Special training or skills/abilities: _____

_____

Favorite classes, subjects and school activities: _____

_____

Social/leisure activities: _____

_____

Additional or supplemental information: _____

_____

References

Name _____

Address _____

Telephone number _____

Name _____

Address _____

Telephone number _____

Name _____

Address _____

Telephone number _____

Name _____

Address _____

Telephone number _____

Final Interviewing Tips

Preparation
- Learn something about the company.
- Have a specific job or jobs in mind.
- Fill in career passport and review it.
- Be prepared to answer questions about yourself.

Appearance
- Well groomed: Neat and clean.
- Suitably dressed.
- Good attitude: Be polite.

Tests
- Listen to instructions.
- Read each question through.
- Write clearly and legibly.

Interview
- Be prompt.
- Answer questions directly and truthfully.
- Go to the interview alone.
- Be well mannered.
- Use good grammar.
- Be enthusiastic and cooperative.
- Don't be afraid to ask questions.

self-image of clients who may have not done well in education or feel they have little to offer to an employer in the way of relevant experiences. Filling out the passport often results in clients being amazed and pleased that they have done so much. Seeing what they have accomplished can make them more confident.

The career passport also can be a valuable tool in the job search. It can be mutually beneficial to both the clients and employers. It helps clients because it can provide a way for them to present themselves more effectively during an interview. It provides a service to employers who might otherwise overlook qualified applicants.

You can use the career passport as a career counseling tool. You can use it to help clients identify and highlight their strengths as well as the gaps in their experiences. It also can serve as a vehicle to discuss such specifics as job application procedures and interviews as well as topics such as the local labor market and the employment prospects within various occupations.

In summary, the career passport is a useful instrument that can benefit clients, employers, and counselors in the following ways:

For clients it can:

- Identify and organize employability skills, work-related attitudes, and abilities in a format that can be updated and revised at any time
- Increase knowledge of work-relevant attitudes and interests
- Improve education and career planning
- Increase self-confidence and self-awareness through self-evaluation
- Produce a comprehensive listing of clients' experiences as a means of introducing themselves to employers
- Develop an understanding by clients of how various experiences can be translated into job-related attitudes and skills
- Provide incentives to clients for acquiring new and different kinds of experiences

For employers it can:

- Provide better information for screening and selecting employees
- Improve their interviews with prospective employees
- Increase their recognition of skill development through work and nonwork experience
- Change employers' attitudes about youth as potential employees
- Supplement and support standard job application procedures with information on individuals' nonwork experience
- Provide a quick picture of a potential employee's job readiness
- Ensure that employers do not overlook qualified people who cannot present themselves effectively in traditional ways

For counselors it can:

- Provide a guide and process that can serve as a counseling tool
- Enhance the content of existing career assessment and counseling programs
- Provide a career passport as an end-product of a classroom unit or training or counseling program
- Provide a counseling tool for developing career, education, or training plans

SOME CLOSING THOUGHTS

This chapter opened with, "Our task is to teach people the skills they need to manage their own careers" (Wilhelm, 1983, p. 12). Often we begin this task by doing career counseling. Relationship development, interviewing, testing, diagnosis, problem specification, clarification, and resolution are part of this process. Unfortunately, we often stop when we have completed these steps thinking that we have completed our work. There is one more step that may need to be completed, however, before this task is achieved and that step is providing our clients with ways of organizing and using self- and environmental information.

The individual career plan forms and formats discussed in this chapter provide several examples of ways to organize and use information. If these examples fit the needs of your clients, they can be adopted for use. More than likely, however, these examples will need to be adapted by modifying the example forms and formats to fit the specific needs of your clients. Occasionally, you and your clients will need to create the individual career plan forms and formats that are needed. The discussion of plan characteristics presented at the beginning of this chapter may be helpful as guidelines to consider in the plan creation process.

REFERENCES

BARTON, S. L., *Career Passports: The Job Connection.* Washington, D.C.: National Institute for Work and Learning, 1981.
GYSBERS, N. C., *Create and Use an Individual Career Plan.* Columbus, Ohio: The National Center for Research in Vocational Education, 1985.
WILHELM, W., "Career Development in Changing Times," *Career Planning and Adult Development Journal,* 1, no. 1 (1983), 9–14.

Career Counseling:
Putting It All Together

*Career counseling, like counseling in general, requires the
counselor to identify properly and respond appropriately to
feelings, thoughts, attitudes, and behaviors expressed by the client
and to assist the client in developing desired and appropriate
behaviors that reflect the increased understanding and insight
resulting from counseling. Further, it requires the counselor to
be competent in assisting the client in acquiring, processing, and
applying information and skills required in effective decision
making and subsequent implementation of plans. (Isaacson,
1985, p. 98)*

In the Introduction to this book a framework for ca-
reer counseling was presented to help you review and examine the selected
career counseling skills and techniques discussed in subsequent chapters.
At this point you have read about skills to understand and interpret certain
kinds of client information and behavior and about skills to analyze and
understand the life career themes that individuals may use to shape and
direct their behavior. In addition, you have read about the uses of three
techniques: the life career assessment, personal styles analysis, and an occupational card sort. Finally, you have read about three types of individual
career plans for use by clients to compile, integrate, and use information
gained during and after career counseling. So far, the focus has been on
specific career counseling skills and techniques. Now the focus shifts to
how these skills and techniques come together in the career counseling
process.

Chapter 7 opens with a review of this framework. Then the phases
and subphases of the career counseling process, as outlined in this framework, are described. As each of the phases and subphases is described, the
skills and techniques presented in this book are discussed briefly as to
where they fit and how they can be used.

CAREER COUNSELING PROCESS

As we stated in the Introduction the career counseling process is envisioned as having two major phases and a number of subphases or elements. In outline form the career counseling process appears as follows:

I. Client goal or problem identification, clarification, and specification.
    A. Establishing a client-counselor relationship including client-counselor responsibilities
    B. Gathering client self- and environmental information to understand the client's goal or problem
        1. Who is the client?
            a. How does the client view himself or herself, others, and his or her world?
            b. What language does the client use to represent these views?
            c. What themes does the client use to organize and direct his or her behavior based on these views?
        2. What is the client's current status and environment like?
            a. Client's life roles, settings, and events
            b. Relationship to client's goal or problem
    C. Understanding client self- and environmental information by sorting, analyzing, and relating such information to client's goal or problem through the use of:
        1. Career development theories
        2. Counseling theories
        3. Classification systems
    D. Drawing conclusions; making diagnoses.
II. Client goal or problem resolution.
    A. Taking action; interventions selected based on diagnoses. Some examples of interventions include counseling techniques, testing, personal styles analyses, career and labor market information, individual career plans, occupational card sorts, and computerized information and decision systems.
    B. Evaluating the impact of the interventions used; did interventions resolve the client's goal or problem?
        1. If goal or problem was not resolved, recycle.
        2. If goal or problem was resolved, close counseling relationship.

Goal or Problem Identification, Clarification, and Specification

This phase of the career counseling process has four subphases or elements: establishing the client-counselor relationship and client-counselor responsibilities, gathering client self- and environment information, understanding client self- and environmental information, and drawing conclusions (making diagnoses). Before these subphases or elements are discussed in detail, however, note the use of the words *goal* or *problem*. Some clients seek help to improve the quality of their lives. No problems are present; the client has a goal of self-improvement. Other clients may be in difficulty, have problems, and need and want assistance to solve them. The point is that you start where your clients are. Do not assume that there is a problem when none may exist. Some clients want information only, not counseling. Other clients may ask for information initially but then move to a particular problem that is troubling them. There is an initial testing time to check you out to see if it is safe to discuss a problem.

Sometimes goal or problem identification is straightforward. A client wants information about jobs in the local labor market because he or she wants fo find a higher paying job. No feelings of anxiety, insecurity, or frustration are evident. At other times problem or goal identification is more complex. The need for information about jobs may be mixed with emotional issues relating to family pressures or personal concerns about self-worth. The focus is on both personal-emotional concerns and career concerns. The distinction made between personal-emotional and career concerns that sometimes appears in the literature and in practice is a false dichotomy.

Establishing the Client-Counselor Relationship. If there is a single concept that is generally agreed on in counseling literature, it is that a positive, productive relationship between client and counselor is a basic and necessary condition if counseling is to be effective. Because much has been written about the characteristics of such a relationship and the skills counselors need to bring it about, we will not discuss these characteristics and skills here (see, for example, Ivey and Simek-Downing, 1980; and Brammer and Shostrom, 1982). It is important to remember, however, that listening and empathizing skills are especially important, as is the need to show clients that we are interested in their needs, concerns, and possibilities. It also is important to remember that once positive, productive relationships are established, they need to be nurtured throughout the duration of the career counseling process.

Finally, this is the time when the nature, structure, and possible results of the career counseling process are discussed with clients. What are the client's expectations? In what time frame is the client working? What can be expected realistically? What responsibility does the client have in the relationship? These and similar questions need to be raised and addressed so that you and your clients can reach a common understanding concerning the nature, structure, and expected results of career counseling.

Gathering Client Self- and Environmental Information. At the same time that a relationship is being established, the task of gathering information begins. This is necessary to understand the goal or problem the client wants to work on or for which the client is being referred. Kinnier and Krumboltz (1984) point out that although the way this is done varies with counselor style and theoretical orientation, the opening questions are similar: "Who are you? What is troubling you? Why have you decided to seek counseling now? Tell me more about yourself and what you want? and What do you want to gain from counseling?" (p. 308) These are typical opening questions that all counselors ask in one form or another.

Understanding the goal or problem clients want to work on begins with understanding the opening or presenting statement they make. Isaacson suggests that there are three types of presenting statements.*

Type 1 Presenting Statement (uncertain, indefinite)

1. I saw a notice (on the bulletin board) about counseling (in the newspaper)
2. Someone said I could take a test here.
3. My (principal, teacher, friend) sent me for counseling.
4. My spouse and I have split up.

Type 2 Presenting Statement (suggests other problem may be present)

1. My major doesn't seem right for me.
2. I like _____ but I'm not doing well in it.
3. I don't like the (school, major, job) I'm in.
4. There seems to be no job in my field.
5. I think I'm ready to make a change.
6. Every time they fire me they tell me to get some counseling.
7. I don't want to work, but it looks like I'll have to.
8. My job requires more (time, effort, travel, etc.) than I want to give.

Type 3 Presenting Statement (probably career counseling)

1. I want to be sure I'm going into the right field.
2. I can't decide on a (college, major, job).
3. The only jobs I know are _____ and _____ , but I (don't want either, like both) of them.
4. I want a job that involves (interest, activity, value, opportunity), what is there?
5. I don't want to be in the same rut as my (parents, sibling, friend).
6. My children are now in school so I'd like to do something outside of the home.

How do we respond to such presenting statements? There are many ways to do so and most involve asking for more information. A typical counselor lead might be, "Can you tell me more about your concern?" As more information is forthcoming, the task is to understand what this information may mean in the context of who the client is and what the client's environment is like.

The life career assessment (LCA) described in Chapter 3 provides a

---

* L. E. Isaacson, *Basics of Career Counseling* (Newton, Mass.: Allyn and Bacon, 1985), pp. 98, 104–5. Reprinted by permission.

particularly useful structure around which to explore who the client is and what the client's current status and environment are like. As you will recall, the LCA is designed to provide insight into clients' levels of functioning in various life roles as well as to yield information about how they interact with their environment. It is useful because it helps establish the context and background for the client's presenting statements of a goal or problem. For example, suppose your client said in the presenting statement, "I don't like the job I am in." At this point you do not know what this means, so you ask the client to elaborate. You will find that the LCA is an excellent tool for this purpose. You first explain to the client what the structure of the LCA is and its purpose. Then you proceed using the LCA outline. As you work with the LCA, more concise statements of a client's goal or problem often emerge, providing a clearer understanding of the client's goal or problem and the dynamics that may be involved (goal or problem clarification and specification).

Concurrent with or subsequent to the use of the LCA, other assessment procedures such as standardized tests of interests, work values, aptitudes, and career maturity may be used. The advantage of using the LCA first is that it provides a basis for understanding the client's goal or problem as well as for making a decision about what types of standardized tests to use, if any. It also provides the opportunity to assess a client's maturity and readiness to benefit from the use of standardized tests. It does so by helping you understand the nature, amount, and quality of the information and knowledge a client has about himself or herself and his or her environment. As the outline of the LCA is followed, you begin to gain a sense of whether or not a client is well informed and how the client has integrated self- and environmental information. You will also find out if the client lacks or is distorting such information. In addition, you will gain a sense of the client's decision skills and strategies. In effect, you will gain a sense of the client's career maturity through the use of the LCA. This helps remedy, at least in part, the criticism of a major assumption of the traditional matching model of career counseling. The assumption is that clients "who are assessed are all sufficiently mature vocationally to have mature and stable traits" (Super, 1983, p. 557).

The use of the LCA or a similar structured interview also helps respond to the problem of assessment with older clients. Sinick (1984) points out that in working with older clients greater reliance should be placed on work history and life history, interests and activities outside of work, and functional abilities. "Interviews can elicit most of this information and can surpass interest inventories, for example, in tapping duration, intensity, and underlying values. Longitudinal information is, in general, more useful with older persons than cross-sectional test data" (pp. 550–51).

In addition, an interview technique such as the LCA provides a structure for the key processes of listening, understanding, and interpreting to unfold in career counseling. This is important because whatever techniques you use in goal or problem identification, clarification, and specification, the ability to systematically gather, understand, and interpret information clients share and the behavior they exhibit is basic to the entire process. Listening skills are important but more is involved. Listening must be done with understanding so that the information clients present and the behavior they exhibit during goal or problem identification, clarification, and specification can be analyzed and interpreted.

How is such understanding achieved? It is achieved through knowledge of theories of human behavior and growth development. Theories provide the constructs and language to help explain the behavior exhibited by clients. Theories become the lenses through which you examine client behavior to help you form hypotheses about the meanings of the behavior, which, in turn, may help you to better identify and understand clients' goals or problems.

Chapter 1, for example, presents such constructs as transformational errors, irrational beliefs, and distorted thinking and the skills involved in identifying and responding to them. Knowing that such client behaviors may exist and having the language to describe them provides the basis for understanding and interpreting these behaviors. To illustrate, suppose a client makes a presenting statement such as, "I want to be sure I'm going into the right field." One interpretation is that this is a straightforward and sincere statement from a client who is concerned about making a choice. However, it may indicate the presence of an irrational belief (I must be absolutely certain before I can act; I need to be perfect). Having the construct of irrational beliefs in your mind provides you with a way to understand and interpret this client information and behavior that may not have been possible without the construct.

In a similar way Chapter 2 presents ideas about how to identify and analyze life career themes. These ideas are drawn from a number of theories of human behavior and human growth and development. Life career themes are useful constructs in career counseling because they supply a common language to help you and your client understand and interpret the client's behavior; to identify, clarify, and specify the client's goal or problem; and to relate past behavior to present and future goal or problem resolution.

The use of an occupational card sort such as the Missouri Occupational Preference Inventory (MOPI) described in Chapter 5 also is recommended as a technique to bring to the surface and gather together client life career themes. The occupational titles serve as stimuli for clients to talk about themselves, others, and the world in which they live as they see it. In a similar way, personal styles analysis, as described in Chapter 4, can be used at this point in career counseling to do the same thing. Both techniques are useful in helping identify client life career themes.

Drawing Conclusions: Making Diagnoses. As you are gathering, understanding, and interpreting client information and behavior during career counseling, you begin to draw tentative conclusions about the meaning of such information and behavior. These tentative conclusions are called diagnoses. Conclusions or diagnoses made initially are not one-time labels applied for all time. They are, instead, more like hypotheses that you substantiate, modify, or discard as the career counseling process unfolds.

Crites (1981) suggests that there are three types of diagnoses that you may want to consider making: differential, dynamic, and decisional. *Differential diagnosis* is the identification and categorization of client goals or problems. Categories such as undecided, indecisive, and incongruent are often used. While differential diagnosis answers the question, "What is the client's problem or goal?" *dynamic diagnosis* focuses on why—on what is going on. The focus is on determining the causes or reasons for the client's problem or goal. For example, a client, differentially diagnosed as undecided, may lack information, whereas a client diagnosed as indecisive may have anxiety and self-doubts and hold a number of irrational beliefs. In the latter case the use of information alone may not be sufficient. In *decisional diagnosis* attention turns to clients' approaches to decision making. It focuses on understanding the processes and sequences clients use to arrive at choices. In this type of diagnosis clients are assessed as to their use of (or lack of use of) decision-making strategies.

A useful tool in determining possible diagnoses, whatever the types, is a classification system of possible client goals or problems. Campbell and Cellini (1981) developed such a system based on an extensive review of the literature. It contains four major career problem categories: decision making, implementing plans, organizational/institutional performance, and organizational/institutional adaptation. Under each are listings of specific career development problems. The authors point out that a career development problem can arise when a client experiences difficulty in completing tasks or does not even try to complete them. The complete classification system is given in Table 7–1.

Another useful tool in determining possible diagnoses is My Vocational Situation (Holland, Daiger, and Power, 1980). It is based on the assumption that career goals or problems can be classified as problems of identity, lack of information, and environmental or personal barriers. The manual suggests that My Vocational Situation can be used for "assessing a client's need for vocational assistance and for assigning clients to two or three kinds of treatments: (1) those for clients with a poor sense of identity who need experience, career seminars, personal counseling, (2) those for clients with a sense of identity who need only information and reassurance, and (3) those for clients who exhibit a combination of these needs" (Holland, Daiger, and Power, 1980, p. 7).

TABLE 7–1   Diagnostic Taxonomy Outline: Problem Categories and Subcategories

1.0. Problems in career decision making
   1.1. Getting started
     A. Lack of awareness of the need for a decision
     B. Lack of knowledge of the decision-making process
     C. Awareness of the need to make a decision, but avoidance of asuming personal responsibility for decision making
   1.2. Information gathering
     A. Inadequate, contradictory, and/or insufficient information
     B. Information overload, i.e., excessive information which confuses the decision maker
     C. Lack of knowledge as to how to gather information, i.e., where to obtain information, how to organize, and to evaluate it
     D. Unwillingness to accept the validity of the information because it does not agree with the person's self-concept.
   1.3. Generating, evaluating, and selecting alternatives
     A. Difficulty deciding due to multiple career options, i.e., too many equally attractive career choices
     B. Failure to generate sufficient career options due to personal limitations such as health, resources, ability, and education
     C. The inability to decide due to the thwarting effects of anxiety such as fear of failure in attempting to fulfill the choice, fear of social disapproval, and/ or fear of commitment to a course of action
     D. Unrealistic choice, i.e., aspiring either too low or too high, based upon criteria such as aptitudes, interests, values, resources, and personal circumstances
     E. Interfering personal constraints which impede a choice such as interpersonal influences and conflicts, situational circumstances, resources, and health
     F. The inability to evaluate alternatives due to lack of knowledge of the evaluation criteria—the criteria could include values, interests, aptitudes, skills, resources, health, age, and personal circumstances.
   1.4. Formulating plans to implementing decisions
     A. Lack of knowledge of the necessary steps to formulate a plan
     B. Inability to utilize a future time perspective in planning
     C. Unwillingness and/or inability to acquire the necessary information to formulate a plan
2.0. Problems in implementing career plans
   2.1. Characteristics of the individual
     A. Failure of the individual to undertake the steps necessary to implement his/her plan
     B. Failure or inability to successfully complete the steps necessary for goal attainment
     C. Adverse changes in the individual's physical or emotional condition
   2.2. Characteristics external to the individual
     A. Unfavorable economic, social, and cultural conditions
     B. Unfavorable conditions in the organization or institution central to the implementation of one's plans
     C. Adverse conditions of or changes in the individual's family situation

3.0. Problems in organization/institutional performance
  3.1. Deficiencies in skills, abilities, and knowledge
    A. Insufficient skills, abilities, and/or knowledge upon position entry, i.e., underqualified to perform satisfactorily
    B. The deterioration of skills, abilities, and/or knowledge over time in the position due to temporary assignment to another position, leave, and/or lack of continual practice of skill
    C. The failure to modify or update skills, abilities, and/or knowledge to stay abreast of job changes, i.e., job obsolescence due to new technology, tools, and knowledge
  3.2. Personal factors
    A. Personality characteristics discrepant with the job, e.g., values, interests, and work habits
    B. Debilitating physical and/or emotional disorders
    C. Adverse off-the-job personal circumstances and/or stressors, e.g., family pressures, financial problems, and personal conflicts
    D. The occurrence of interpersonal conflicts on the job which are specific to performance requirements, e.g., getting along with the boss, co-workers, customers, and clients
  3.3. Conditions of the organization/institutional environment
    A. Ambiguous or inappropriate job requirements, e.g., lack of clarity of assignments, work overload, and conflicting assignments
    B. Deficiencies in the operational structure of the organization/institution
    C. Inadequate support facilities, supplies, and resources, e.g., insufficient lighting, ventilation, tools, support personnel, and materials
    D. Insufficient reward system, e.g., compensation, fringe benefits, status, recognition, and opportunities for advancement
4.0. Problems in organizational/institutional adaptation
  4.1. Initial entry
    A. Lack of knowledge of organizational rules and procedures
    B. Failure to accept or adhere to organizational rules and procedures
    C. Inability to assimilate large quantities of new information, i.e., information overload
    D. Discomfort in a new geographic location
    E. Discrepancies between the individual's expectations and the realities of the institutional/organizational evnironment
  4.2. Changes over time
    A. Changes over the life span in one's attitudes, values, life style, career plans, or commitment to the organization which lead to incongruence between the individual and the environment
    B. Changes in the organizational/institutional environment which lead to incongruence between the individual and the environment, e.g., physical and administrative structure, policies, and procedures
  4.3. Interpersonal relationships
    A. Interpersonal conflicts arising from differences of opinion, style, values, mannerisms, etc.
    B. The occurrence of verbal or physical abuse or sexual harrassment

Source: R. E. Campbell and J. V. Cellini, "A Diagnostic Taxonomy of Adult Career Problems," *Journal of Vocational Behavior,* 19 (1981), 179–80. Reprinted with permission.

In addition to considering these classification systems you may wish to read the chapter on "Diagnosis and Treatment of Vocational Problems" by Rounds and Tinsley in the *Handbook of Counseling Psychology* for information about other possible classification systems. They group such systems into three broad categories: descriptive, psychodynamic, and developmental classifications. Within each category they discuss specific systems. At the end of their discussion of classification systems they make the following point:

> Failure to identify, define, and categorize vocational problems adversely affects the practice of and research on career interventions by promoting poor communication among practitioners, precluding meaningful comparisons of career interventions, failing to obtain basic descriptive data about the prevalence of and prognosis for specific vocational problems, and generally encouraging uncritical thinking about career interventions. (Rounds and Tinsley, 1984, p. 157)

Client Goal or Problem Resolution

Taking Action. The reason for identifying, clarifying, and specifying clients' goals or problems is to find ways to resolve them through appropriate interventions. Once clients become aware of the nature of their goals or problems, the focus of career assessment and counseling turns to you and your clients becoming actively involved in goal or problem solutions (Crites, 1981). Here the keys are the diagnoses or tentative conclusions reached as to the nature and structure of the goals or problems, because the diagnoses made determine the choices of interventions that are to be used. How does the connection between diagnoses and interventions work? Let us look at some examples using illustrations from the career counseling models of Crites (1981), Kinnier and Krumboltz (1984), and Super (1983, 1984) described previously.

Crites (1981) identifies and describes three types of diagnoses: differential, dynamic, and decisional. He also suggests three broad outcomes for career counseling: making a career choice, aquisition of decisional skills, and enhanced general adjustment. With these elements in mind, suppose a client's problem was identified as difficulty in making a career choice. Also suppose that the diagnoses were that the client was (1) undecided (differential diagnosis); (2) had not been exposed to much in the way of information about occupations while growing up, and as a result, had a very limited view of the occupational alternatives available (dynamic diagnosis); and (3) lacked some basic skills about how to gather and analyze information (decisional diagnosis). To reach a resolution of the client's problem, now clarified and specified through the above diagnoses, Crites (1981) suggests that, used separately or in combination, interview techniques, test interpretation, and career and labor market information are possible intervention strategies. Based on the above diagnoses career and labor market informa-tion can be used to inform and instruct the client about the realities and possibilities of the work world. The client may be motivated to explore new options as information opens up new possibilities. Interest inventories and aptitude tests can help provide comparisons with people in occupations. Similarly, personal styles analysis (Chapter 4) can be used to help the client relate his or her personal style to the styles of people in occupations. Coun-seling (listening, reflecting, providing information, confronting, teaching) can help the client sort out and bring together career and labor market information and test and styles analyses results into a meaningful gestalt so that a decision can be made about a career choice.

For Kinnier and Krumboltz (1984) the connection between diagnoses and interventions is tied to what they identify as six basic obstacles to career fulfillment. These obstacles can be viewed as six possible diagnostic catego-ries into which clients' goals or problems can be classified. (As with most classification systems, more than one category can and probably should be used.) Based on the category or categories chosen the counseling tasks that need to be accomplished are identified. Table 7–2 illustrates this relation-ship.

Suppose that as a part of the goal or problem identification, clarifica-tion, and specification process it becomes apparent that inaccurate infor-mation and maladaptive beliefs play a part in the client's perception of self and the work world and that this perception seems to interfere with mak-ing a decision about which job to take after graduation. The task for the counselor in this situation is to begin restructuring those faulty beliefs, perhaps by using cognitive restructuring interventions such as those identi-fied by Keller, Biggs, and Gysbers (1982). In a similar manner, if a client is diagnosed as being uncertain about priorities and values and it is decided that some ordering and understanding of values are necessary prerequi-

TABLE 7–2 Relationship between Client Obstacles and Counseling Tasks

CLIENT OBSTACLES	COUNSELING TASKS
Inaccurate information/maladaptive beliefs	Cognitive restructuring
Uncertain priorities and values	Clarify values
Unaware of abilities, interests, and skills	Self-assessment of career relevent attributes
Wealth of occupational information	Obtain information gathering and analyzing skills
Lack of systematic career decision skills	Obtain career decision skills
Lack of job-seeking skills	Obtain job-seeking skills

Source: Adapted with permission from R. T. Kinnier and J. D. Krumboltz, "Procedures for Successful Career Counseling," in *Designing Careers: Counseling to Enhance Education, Work, and Leisure,* eds. N. C. Gysbers and associates (San Francisco: Jossey-Bass, 1984), pp. 307–35.

sites for making an occupational choice, then appropriately selected intervention strategies to clarify values will need to be used.

In Super's model (1984) the assessment phase focuses first on interviewing and assembling the data on hand. Then specific attention is devoted to work salience, career maturity, self-concepts, and interests and abilities. This is followed by a review of all data, matching and predicting, and counseling (Table 7–3).

In illustrating the connection between diagnoses and interventions using Super's model of career counseling, suppose that on completion of the first step with a client (assembling the data available, conducting an interview, and conducting a preliminary assessment), the client's expressed goal is tentatively diagnosed as the need to make an occupational choice. The client is a college junior and is feeling the need to choose an occupa-

TABLE 7–3   A Developmental Assessment Model

Step I. Preview
A. Assembly of data on hand
B. Intake interview
C. Preliminary assessment

Step II. Depth-View: Further Testing?
A. Work salience
    1. Relative importance of diverse roles
        a. Study
        b. Work and career
        c. Home and family
        d. Community service
        e. Leisure activities
    2. Values sought in each role
B. Career maturity
    1. Planfulness
    2. Exploratory attitudes
    3. Decision-making skills
    4. Information
        a. World of work
        b. Preferred occupational group
        c. Other life-career roles
    5. Realism
C. Self-concepts
    1. Self-esteem
    2. Clarity
    3. Harmony
    4. Cognitive complexity
    5. Realism
    6. Others (Super and others 1963)
D. Level of abilities and potential functioning
E. Field of interest and probable activity

tion fairly soon that is related to his or her major. Before moving directly ahead with intervention strategies to help the client such as this achieve this goal, Super suggests that additional assessment may be needed. Is the client mature enough to have mature interests and values? Is the client "planful enough to benefit from the review of aptitude, interest, and value data for educational and vocational planning" (Super, 1983, p. 557)?

To answer questions such as these, Super proposes in his second step, to do an in-depth assessment of the client's feelings and thoughts about the importance of work in relationship to other life roles (work salience). He also proposes in-depth assessments of the client's career maturity and the nature and condition of the client's self-concept. Such assessment, he points out, can provide the basis for making diagnoses about a client's level of knowledge, readiness, and motivation to engage in educational and occupational decision making.

Step III. Assessment of All Data
A. Review of all data
B. Matching and prediction
   1. Individual and occupations
   2. Individual and nonoccupational roles
C. Planning communication with counselee, family, and others
Step IV. Counseling
A. Joint review and discussion
B. Revision or acceptance of assessment
C. Assimilation by the counselee
   1. Understanding the present and next stages
   2. Recognizing one's self-concepts
      a. Accepting the actual
      b. Clarifying the actual and the ideal
      c. Developing harmony among self-concepts
      d. Refining cognitive complexity
      e. Assuring the realism of self-concepts
      f. Others
   3. Matching self and occupations
   4. Understanding the meaning of life roles
   5. Exploration for maturing?
   6. Exploring the breadth for crystallization?
   7. Exploration in depth for specification?
   8. Choice of preparation, training, or jobs?
   9. Searches for outlets for self-realization?
D. Discussion of action implications and planning
   1. Planning
   2. Execution
   3. Follow-up for support and evaluation

Source: D. E. Super "Career and Life Development," in *Career Choice and Development,* eds. D. Brown, L. Brooks, and associates (San Francisco: Jossey-Bass, 1984), pp. 224–25. Reprinted with permission.

Suppose that as a result of such an assessment it is found that the client has not yet made much of an investment in the work role; has little knowledge about what is involved in occupational exploration, planning, and decision making; and has low self-esteem. Before attention is given to helping a client make a specific occupational decision, interventions may be needed to help him or her gain a more complete perspective of the work role; come to an understanding of the importance of planning and decision making and to gain the necessary skills to do planning and decision making; and enhance the client's self-concept.

Developing an Individual Career Plan.   At this point in the career assessment and counseling process clients may need a vehicle to organize and relate the self-environmental, and career and labor market information they have gathered. One of the plans described in Chapter 6 or one developed especially for a particular client using the concepts discussed in Chapter 6 can be used. Once clients begin gathering and organizing information in plan form, it can become a vehicle for them to relate and apply the information they have gathered and organized to their career planning and decision making. They may find that by putting information together in certain ways and in certain categories, relationships become apparent that were not apparent before. Self-appraisal information and experience auditing and cataloging often can be translated directly into job-related knowledge, attitudes, and skills. When these relationships are seen, client self-confidence and self-worth may be increased.

Evaluating the Impact of Interventions and Closing the Counseling Relationship.   During the goal or problem identification, clarification, and specification stage you and your client determine what the client's goal or problem is. During goal or problem resolution a decision is made about appropriate interventions to attain the client's goal or alleviate the problem. The final phase of goal or problem resolution is assessing changes that may have occurred and evaluating the impact of the interventions used. One way to accomplish this is to have the client review and summarize what has taken place during the career counseling process. Then you can add your own review and summary.

During the summary you and your client may find that there is some unfinished business remaining. Your client may need more information or more time to consider and reflect on the information already available. As a result you may recycle back to the same interventions to allow more time for consideration and reflections or you may try other interventions.

Also during the summary you may find that your client is unsure about whether or not he or she is ready to close the counseling relationship. If you sense the client's hesitation, feelings of insecurity need to be addressed. You may want to open up this topic by saying, "It seems as if we have achieved what we wanted to achieve during our time together. Sometimes when people reach this point, having made some of the changes you have made, they wonder if they are ready to handle new situations. Could it be that you feel this way?" If you sense this is the case with your client, these feelings need to be addressed directly as a part of closing the career counseling process. Part of closing the process is working through any emotional investment associated with the career counseling relationship (Brammer and Shostrom, 1982).

REFERENCES

BRAMMER, L. M., and SHOSTROM, E. L., *Therapeutic Psychology* (4th ed.). Englewood Cliffs, N.J.: Prentice-Hall, 1982.

CAMPBELL, R. E., and CELLINI, J. V., "A Diagnostic Taxomy of Adult Career Problems," *Journal of Vocational Behavior*, 19 (1981), 175–90.

CRITES, J. O., *Career Counseling: Models, Methods, and Materials*. New York: McGraw-Hill, 1981.

ISAACSON, L. E., *Basics of Career Counseling*. Newton, Mass.: Allyn and Bacon, 1985.

IVEY, A. E., and SIMEK-DOWNING, L., *Counseling and Psychotherapy*. Englewood Cliffs, N.J.: Prentice-Hall, 1980.

HOLLAND, J. L., DAIGER, D. C., and POWER, P. G., *My Vocational Situation Manual*. Palo Alto, Calif.: Consulting Psychologists Press, 1980.

KELLER, K. E., BIGGS, D. A., and GYSBERS, N. C., "Career Counseling from a Cognitive Perspective," *The Personnel and Guidance Journal*, 60 (1982).

KINNIER, R. T., and KRUMBOLTZ, J. D., "Procedures for Successful Career Counseling," in *Designing Careers: Counseling to Enhance Education, Work, and Leisure*, eds. N. C. Gysbers and associates. San Francisco: Jossey-Bass, 1984.

ROUNDS, J. B., JR., and TINSLEY, H. E. A., "Diagnosis and Treatment of Vocational Problems," in *Handbook of Counseling Psychology*, eds. S. D. Brown and R. W. Lent. New York: John Wiley, 1984.

SINICK, D., "Problems of Work and Retirement for an Aging Population," in *Designing Careers: Counseling to Enhance Education, Work, and Leisure*, eds. N. C. Gysbers and associates. San Francisco: Jossey-Bass, 1984.

SUPER, D. E., "Assessment in career guidance: Toward Truly Developmental Counseling," *The Personnel and Guidance Journal*, 61 (1983), 555–62.

———, "Career and Life Development," in *Career Choice and Development*, eds. D. Brown, L. Brooks, and associates. San Francisco: Jossey-Bass, 1984.

Index